CHE GUEVARA TALKS TO YOUNG PEOPLE

TITLES IN THIS SERIES
edited and introduced by Mary-Alice Waters

Our History Is Still Being Written
BY ARMANDO CHOY, GUSTAVO CHUI, MOISÉS SÍO WONG (2005)

Aldabonazo
BY ARMANDO HART (2004)

Marianas in Combat
BY TETÉ PUEBLA (2003)

October 1962: The 'Missile' Crisis as Seen from Cuba
BY TOMÁS DIEZ (2002)

From the Escambray to the Congo
BY VÍCTOR DREKE (2002)

Playa Girón/Bay of Pigs
BY FIDEL CASTRO AND JOSÉ RAMÓN FERNÁNDEZ (2001)

Cuba and the Coming American Revolution
BY JACK BARNES (2001)

Fertile Ground: Che Guevara and Bolivia
BY RODOLFO SALDAÑA (2001)

Che Guevara Talks to Young People (2000)

Making History
BY NÉSTOR LÓPEZ CUBA, ENRIQUE CARRERAS,
JOSÉ RAMÓN FERNÁNDEZ, HARRY VILLEGAS (1999)

Pombo: A Man of Che's guerrilla
BY HARRY VILLEGAS (1997)

Episodes of the Cuban Revolutionary War, 1956–58,
BY ERNESTO CHE GUEVARA (1996)

The Bolivian Diary of Ernesto Che Guevara (1994)

To Speak the Truth
BY FIDEL CASTRO AND ERNESTO CHE GUEVARA (1992)

How Far We Slaves Have Come!
BY NELSON MANDELA AND FIDEL CASTRO (1991)

U.S. Hands Off the Mideast!
BY FIDEL CASTRO AND RICARDO ALARCÓN (1990)

In Defense of Socialism
BY FIDEL CASTRO (1989)

CHE GUEVARA TALKS TO YOUNG PEOPLE

❦

Preface by Armando Hart Dávalos

Introduction by Mary-Alice Waters

Pathfinder

NEW YORK   LONDON   MONTREAL   SYDNEY

Edited by Mary-Alice Waters

ISBN 978-0-87348-911-9
Library of Congress Catalog Card Number 99-76024
Manufactured in the United States

First edition, 2000
Seventh printing, 2009

TEXT: Spanish text of speeches by Ernesto Che Guevara assembled and
   digital file compiled by Casa Editora Abril.
COVER PHOTO: Che Guevara addressing First Latin American Youth
   Conference in Havana, July 28, 1960. (Osvaldo Salas)
COVER DESIGN: Eric Simpson
BOOK DESIGN: Eva Braiman

Pathfinder
www.pathfinderpress.com
E-mail: pathfinder@pathfinderpress.com

CONTENTS

ERNESTO CHE GUEVARA

Ernesto "Che" Guevara was born in Rosario, Argentina, on June 14, 1928. Both before and after graduating from medical school in 1953, he traveled extensively throughout Latin America. While living in Guatemala in 1954, he joined with others in opposing the CIA's operation to overthrow the government of Jacobo Arbenz. Following the ouster of Arbenz, Guevara, like thousands of others, made his way across the border to Mexico. There, in the summer of 1955, he was introduced to Fidel Castro. He and Raúl Castro became the first two members selected by Fidel for the expeditionary force being organized by the Cuban July 26 Revolutionary Movement to overthrow dictator Fulgencio Batista.

In late November 1956 eighty-two combatants set sail from Tuxpan, Mexico, aboard the yacht *Granma*. The rebel forces landed on Cuba's southeastern coast in Oriente province on December 2 to begin the revolutionary war from the Sierra Maestra mountains. Originally the troop doctor, Guevara was named commander of the second Rebel Army column (Column no. 4) in July 1957. At the end of August 1958 he led "Ciro Redondo" Column no. 8 toward Las Villas province in central Cuba. The Las Villas campaign culminated in the capture of Santa Clara, Cuba's third-largest city, and sealed the fate of the dictatorship.

Following Batista's fall on January 1, 1959, Guevara carried a number of responsibilities in the new revolutionary government, including head of the Department of Industrialization of the National Institute of Agrarian Reform (INRA), president of the National Bank, and minister of industry, while continuing his duties as an officer in the Rebel Army and then the Revolutionary Armed Forces. He frequently represented Cuba internationally, including at a meeting sponsored by the Organization of American States in Punta del Este, Uruguay, in 1961; at the United Nations in December 1964; and in other world forums. As a leader of the July 26 Movement, he helped bring about the unification of the July 26 Movement, Popular Socialist Party, and March 13 Revolutionary Directorate in a single political organization, a process that culminated in the founding of the Communist Party of Cuba in October 1965.

After nine years of outstanding service in the leadership of the revolution—and consistent with a long-standing agreement with Fidel Castro—in March 1965 Guevara resigned his government and party posts, including his military commission and responsibilities, and left Cuba to continue fighting imperialism "in other lands." Along with a number of Cuban internationalist volunteers, some of whom would later join him in Bolivia, Guevara went first to the Congo to aid the movement founded by Patrice Lumumba, leader of the Congolese struggle for independence from Belgium. From November 1966 to October 1967 he led a guerrilla campaign in Bolivia against that country's military dictatorship, seeking to link up with rising revolutionary struggles by workers and peasants throughout the region. Wounded and captured in the Yuro Ravine on October 8, 1967, by the Bolivian army in an operation organized together with the CIA, he was murdered the following day in the town of La Higuera.

PREFACE

Writing a preface to *Che Guevara Talks to Young People*—which has as an afterword Fidel's speech at the monument built in the center of the island to house the hero's sacred remains, together with those of his unforgettable comrades—constitutes for me both an honor and a genuine challenge. I will try to share with the young reader—to whom this book is largely directed—some necessarily brief thoughts on this outstanding figure of the Americas and of contemporary world history.

It's true that Che would speak much differently to young people today, who are living under very different conditions, than he did over three decades ago. Nevertheless, in rereading these talks, one is struck by how extremely relevant they are. These speeches confirm that Che is indeed a man of the present.

At the beginning of the 1990s it was said that all models for changing the world had disappeared, together with the possibility of finding new ones. The image of the Heroic Guerrilla, however, rises throughout the Western world as a specter that continues to grow. And it will do so, with greater or lesser force and richness of ideas, to the extent that it reaches young people and they take up the essential part of his actions and aspirations.

José Carlos Mariátegui, one of Latin America's great revolutionary thinkers, studied and pointed to the need for myths. He pointed out how peoples who have accomplished great feats have had to create myths among the masses. If we want to be revolutionaries in the strict sense of the word, we must study the reasons and the factors for why Che lives on in the hearts of the Americas and expresses, in a thousand different ways, the desires and aspirations of the most radical youth on various continents. Thirty-some years after his rise to immortality in the Yuro Ravine, his image resonates through plazas and streets, reviving his cry of "Ever onward to victory!" Finding the reasons behind these facts is the best way to uphold the ideas of socialism and the possibilities of revolutionary change.

The teachings and the example of Che's sacrifice in the jungles of Bolivia have etched in the minds of the new generations for all time a sense of heroism, and of moral values in politics and history. And since the moral factor has been what's lacking in politics and has ended up leading to revolutions, there is one conviction of Che's that has been dramatically confirmed: without the moral factor, there is no revolution. He also spoke with eloquence, depth, and rigor about the need for a new man in the twenty-first century. Life itself has compelled this individual to be formed in the twentieth century. Recognizing the enormous role of culture and moral values in the history of civilization, and extracting from it the necessary practical consequences is Commander Ernesto Che Guevara's most important message to young people. There is a history behind this. Civilization never made an analysis with the necessary depth, from a scientific viewpoint, of the role of moral and spiritual values over the course of history. That is the most important intellectual challenge that the twentieth century has left to youth.

In Europe, Western and Christian culture began to evolve before the year 1000 until it achieved, with Marx and Engels, the highest level of philosophic knowledge in relation to social and economic science. In Latin America and the Caribbean, meanwhile, a line of thinking crystallized—symbolized by Bolívar and Martí—that, on a scientific basis, emphasized the power of man and the role of education, culture, and politics. The originality of Ernesto Che Guevara—as with the Cuban Revolution—consists of the following: Inspired by the spiritual heritage of Our America, and starting with his commitment to moral values, he adopted the ideas of Marx and Engels, and advocated using the so-called subjective factors to motivate and guide the revolutionary action of the masses and of society as a whole.

What is valuable and of interest from the standpoint of Marxism is that from this vantage point, Che got radically closer to Marx than did other interpretations of the ideas of the author of *Capital* that were prevalent during the second half of the twentieth century. The Third World perspective of the internationalist guerrilla fighters who fell in Bolivia was an implicit call to socialists to decisively orient their actions toward the Third World. The wisdom of this political and moral course was not understood and supported at the time by those who could and should have done so. For this reason, the world changed along lines favorable to the most reactionary right, ending up in postmodern chaos.

In Che's speech in Algiers on February 24, 1964, this call took on a dramatic and polemical character. Tragically, history would prove who was right. The saddest thing for revolutionaries is that Che's position on the role of the previously colonized or neocolonized countries was closely in line with what Lenin had brilliantly foreseen decades earlier, pointing to the importance of liberation movements that were emerging in the East. Valuable literature exists by the person who forged the October Revolution, and it should be restudied at the present time.

The inadequacy of the social sciences under the prevailing system stems from the fact that they ignore one decisive reality: today's growing poverty, the root of the evils and anguish suffered by modern man, together with the destruction of nature. Overcoming this situation is man's greatest challenge as the twenty-first century dawns. From the scientific viewpoint, taking up this issue—rather than pretending it doesn't exist—is the essence of an ethical system that aspires to be built on solid foundations for the future. Ignoring human pain is the great crime of the social systems that currently exist. We are realists, but for us the reality of man is complete and whole, not partial and mean, which is the way the existing interests see reality.

Che saw and appraised reality from an ethical standpoint—in order to improve it. That is where the power of the myth he left us resides. His ideas combine the most advanced thinking of European philosophical thought—Marx and Engels—with the utopian vision of Our America—Bolívar and Martí.

The error of those who renounce utopia is in not considering the real needs that emerge from the facts that lie beneath the surface. For this reason, they are unable to conceive of tomorrow's truths.

The essence of the Latin American culture present in Che's revolutionary ideas consists of viewing reality and the effort to change it as indispensable elements for understanding truth and transforming the world in the interests of justice, while at the same time taking the New World's utopian sense and converting it into an incentive for forging tomorrow's reality. Che did not renounce either reality or hope. He was a revolutionary of science and of conscience, both of which are needed by the Americas and the world in order to confront the challenge we face in the next century.

Study carefully these works by Che and, whether you are students or other youth, you will find a good lesson for the present and for the future.

Armando Hart Dávalos
December 1999

INTRODUCTION

All the members of the Cuban government—young in age, young in character, and young in their illusions—have nevertheless matured in the extraordinary school of experience, in living contact with the needs and aspirations of the people.

> Ernesto Che Guevara
> July 28, 1960

Che Guevara Talks to Young People is not a "Che for Beginners." The legendary Argentine-born revolutionary, who helped lead the first socialist revolution in the Americas and initiate the renewal of Marxism in the 1960s, speaks as an equal with the youth of Cuba and the world. He never talks down. He sets an example as he urges young people to rise to the level of revolutionary activity and scientific thought necessary to confront and resolve the historic contradictions of capitalism that threaten humanity.

He challenges them to work—physically and intellectually. To learn to be disciplined. To become revolutionists of action, fearlessly taking their place in the vanguard on the front lines of struggles, small and large. He urges them, as they grow and change through these experiences, to read widely and study seriously. To absorb, and to make their own, the scientific and cultural achievements not only of their own people but of all previous civilizations. To aspire to be revolutionary combatants, knowing that a different kind of society can be born only out of struggles by men and women ready to put their lives and their lifetimes on the line for it. He appeals to them to politicize the work of the organizations and institutions they are part of, and in the process politicize themselves. To become a different kind of human being as they strive together with working people of all lands to transform the world. And along this line of march, he encourages them to continuously renew and revel in the spontaneity, freshness, optimism, and joy of being young.

"Che was truly a communist," Cuban president Fidel Castro told the solemn assembly in the city of Santa Clara on October 17, 1997, as the remains of Guevara and six of his fellow combatants were interred at the site of a memorial in their honor, thirty years after they fell in combat in Bolivia. Che based himself on objective laws, Castro said, the laws of history, and had unqualified confidence in the capacity of human beings, ordinary working people, to change the course of history. In the process of making a socialist revolution on the doorstep of Yankee imperialism, Che insisted, the workers and peasants of Cuba would remake themselves as social beings with a new consciousness, a new set of values, a new world view, a transformed relationship to one another. They would set an example for all.

In his preface to these speeches, Armando Hart underscores that on this question as on others, Guevara—and the Cuban Revolution he was part of—came "radically closer to Marx" than most of those in the second half of the twentieth century who claimed to speak in the name of communism. "If this revolution is Marxist," Guevara told the nine hundred participants in the First Latin American Youth Congress in the summer of 1960, it is "because it discovered, by its own methods, the road pointed out by Marx." Deeply rooted in the history, culture, and politics of his Latin American homeland, Guevara brought to that social reality and its traditions of struggle a scientific understanding of the universal laws of the history of class societies. He combined a renewal of Marxist orthodoxy in theory with the example of physical and moral courage that earned him the name, the Heroic Guerrilla.

In the pages that follow, Guevara draws frequently on his own experiences to explain to others why the image of the lone, self-sacrificing hero—the image in which many later tried to remake Che himself—is nothing but the exaltation of bourgeois individualism, the flip side of the coin of the dog-eat-dog reality of capitalism. It is the opposite of the revolutionary cooperative course of the toilers, the course that made the Cuban Revolution possible.

Speaking to a group of medical students and health workers in August 1960, Guevara describes how his youthful idealism when he was studying to be a doctor led him to dream of being a famous researcher, "of working tirelessly to achieve something that could really be put at the disposal of humanity, but that would be a personal triumph at the same time. I was, as we all are, a child of my environment."

As he traveled throughout the Americas, however, and learned firsthand of the economic, social, and political realities of imperialist domination, he came to recognize the futility of such a course. "The isolated effort, the individual effort, the purity of ideals, the desire to sacrifice an entire lifetime to the noblest of ideals—all that is for naught if the effort is made alone, solitary, in some corner of Latin America, fighting against hostile governments and social conditions that permit no progress.

"A revolution," Guevara said, "needs what we have in Cuba: an entire people who are mobilized, who have learned the use of arms and the practice of unity in combat."

Before he could be a revolutionary doctor, there was
a revolution to be made. Once set on that line of march,
Guevara never turned back.

From a young student rebel attracted to revolutionary
ideas, Guevara—like other great communist leaders before him, starting with Marx and Engels themselves—was
won to the popular revolutionary vanguard fighting arms
in hand for liberation from oppression, exploitation, and
all the accompanying indignities. Along that trajectory of
revolutionary action by the toilers combined with systematic, disciplined, hard work and study, Guevara emerged as
one of the foremost proletarian leaders of our epoch. The
opening of the first socialist revolution in the Americas,
whose victory Guevara helped to assure, the example of internationalism set by the entire leadership of the revolution,
and Guevara's own contributions captured in speeches and
writings he left us, initiated a renewal of Marxism that was
not limited to the Americas.

By consistently taking the political and theoretical conquests of Marx, Engels, and Lenin as his guide, by making the early years following the October 1917 revolution
a point of reference, Guevara worked to lay a foundation
that would help lead the Cuban Revolution to a different
fate than that suffered by the regimes and parties of Eastern Europe and the Soviet Union. It is no accident that his
name and example are associated so closely with what is
called in Cuba the Rectification process, the policies initiated by Cuban president Fidel Castro in 1986 (well before
"the meringue fell" across Eastern Europe, as Cubans say)
that strengthened Cuban working people and set the revolution on a course enabling it to survive the severe test
of political isolation and economic hardship in the 1990s
known as the Special Period.

Che Guevara's profound Marxism informs every page

of this book. "On the most basic level," he told the international meeting of architecture students in Havana in September 1963, "our country has what is scientifically called the dictatorship of the proletariat, and we do not allow anyone to touch or threaten the state power of the proletarian dictatorship. But within the dictatorship of the proletariat there can be a vast field for discussion and expression of ideas."

As Armando Hart observes, Guevara set the example and tirelessly educated those he influenced, especially young people, on the need for the socialist revolution to take and hold the moral high ground against the old ruling classes who claim to speak in the name of freedom and justice, of beauty and truth. With his trenchant sense of humor, he helped those he worked with comprehend the class character of all such questions.

Among the many delightfully rich moments readers will encounter in the speeches that follow is Guevara's lesson in the practical connection between the class foundations of ethics and aesthetics. Speaking to architecture students in 1963, and explaining that technology is a weapon that serves different classes for different ends, Che pointed to a mural on the wall of the auditorium. He remarked that there is a weapon depicted in the mural, "a U.S.-made M-1, a Garand rifle. When it was in the hands of Batista's soldiers and they were firing on us, that weapon was hideous. But that same weapon became extraordinarily beautiful when we captured it, when we wrested it from a soldier's hands, when it became part of the arsenal of the people's army. In our hands it became an object of dignity."

A similar thread of scientific clarity and an uncompromising dialectical materialism on questions such as education and human nature, links Guevara to fundamental writings of Marx, such as his 1845 "Theses on Feuerbach."

Criticizing the mechanical materialism of some of the pro-
gressive bourgeois forces of the time, Marx wrote: "The
materialist doctrine concerning the changing of circumstances and upbringing forgets that circumstances are
changed by men and that the educator must himself be
educated." Human nature is not an immutable characteristic of human beings considered as abstract individuals, he
said, but concretely "the ensemble of the social relations."

In his farewell remarks to the international volunteer work
brigades, Guevara asks: "Have the people of this country
made a revolution because that's just the way they are?"

"Absolutely not," he answers.

"The people are the way they are because they are in
the midst of a revolution." Through their actions, they
are forging different social relations and a different understanding of themselves and the world—thus becoming
different individuals, creating a different "human nature,"
on the road to becoming socialist men and women.

"We learned to respect the peasant," Guevara told the
Latin American Youth Congress in July 1960. "We learned
to respect his sense of independence, his loyalty; to recognize his age-old yearning for the land that had been
snatched from him; and to recognize his experience in the
thousand paths through the hills.

"And from us, the peasants learned how valuable a man
is when he has a rifle in his hand, and when he is prepared
to fire that rifle at another man, regardless of how many
rifles the other man has. The peasants taught us their
know-how," Guevara said, "and we taught the peasants
our sense of rebellion. And from that moment until today,
and forever, the peasants of Cuba and the rebel forces of
Cuba—today the Cuban revolutionary government—have
marched united as one."

Youth must march in the vanguard, Guevara insists

throughout, taking on the hardest tasks in every endeavor. That is the only road toward becoming leaders of other women and men—just as the officers in the Rebel Army won their stripes on the battlefield. Youth must learn to lead not only their peers, but revolutionists older than themselves as well. You must be a model "for older men and women who have lost some of that youthful enthusiasm, who have lost a certain faith in life, and who always respond well to example," Guevara told the UJC leaders in October 1962.

Above all, you must be political. "To be apolitical is to turn one's back on every movement in the world," he says to the international meeting of architecture students.

And to the youth working at the Ministry of Industry—which he himself headed at the time—Guevara explained the need to "politicize the ministry." That is the only way you can fight to change it from being a "cold, a very bureaucratic place, a nest of nit-picking bureaucrats and bores, from the minister on down, who are constantly tackling concrete tasks in order to search for new relationships and new attitudes," he told them. Only by bringing the broadest world and class perspectives—and the most uncompromising acceptance of the laws of motion of modern history—into the most routine of tasks can you counter the depoliticizing, bureaucratizing pressures of day-to-day existence that can undermine the morale, confidence, and combativity of even the best revolutionary fighters.

No one can be a leader, Guevara told the UJC cadres, "if you think about the revolution only at the moment of decisive sacrifice, at the moment of combat, of heroic adventure, at moments that are out of the ordinary, yet in your work you are mediocre or less than mediocre. How can that be?"

If "politicize the ministry" is one part of the answer he gives, voluntary work is another.

"Why do we emphasize voluntary work so much?" asks Guevara. "Economically it means practically nothing." But it is "important today because these individuals are giving a part of their lives to society without expecting anything in return. . . . This is the first step in transforming work into what it will eventually become, as a result of the advance of technology, the advance of production, and the advance of the relations of production: an activity of a higher level, a social necessity" that we will look forward to in the way we now anticipate a Sunday off.

Along that line of march "you will automatically become the youth's vanguard," Guevara told the UJC members at the Ministry of Industry. You will never have to sit around engaging in theoretical discussions about what youth should be doing. "Stay young, don't transform yourselves into old theoreticians, or theorizers, maintain the freshness and enthusiasm of youth."

≈

The simultaneous publication of *Che Guevara Talks to Young People* in both Spanish and English was made possible by the ample cooperation of Casa Editora Abril, the publishing house of the Union of Young Communists in Cuba, whose director enthusiastically supported the project from its inception in February 1998. He contributed his time and knowledge to help select the texts, as well as to review the annotation and introductory materials. Rafaela Valerino, head of the editorial department at Casa Editora Abril, supervised the preparation of the electronic files of the speeches, and reviewed the entire manuscript. While the efforts of Casa Editora Abril have increased the accuracy and readability of the book, for which we are grateful, Pathfinder takes full responsibility for all the editorial decisions and thus any errors that remain.

Special appreciation is also owed to Aleida March, director of Che's Personal Archive, for her cooperation and insightful suggestions on the selection of both the speeches and photos.

The invaluable photo signature and internal photo pages were assembled with the help and knowledge of Delfín Xiqués of *Granma,* Manuel Martínez of *Bohemia,* and Juan Moreno of *Juventud Rebelde.*

Readers who are unfamiliar with many of the names and historical events referred to throughout will find the glossary notes and list of further reading at the end especially helpful.

~

"To the powerful masters we represent all that is absurd, negative, irreverent, and disruptive in this America that they so despise and scorn," Guevara told the students at the University of Havana in March 1960. But to the great mass of the people of the Americas, "we represent everything noble, sincere and combative."

Forty years later those words continue to ring true. Guevara's talks with young people continue to point the way forward—the way toward becoming revolutionary combatants of the highest caliber, and, in his own words, "politicians of a new type."

Mary-Alice Waters
January 2000

ABOUT THESE SPEECHES

Che Guevara Talks to Young People is being published simultaneously in Spanish and English. All the speeches have appeared previously in Spanish in Cuba, either in *Revolución*, the newspaper of the July 26 Movement, *Granma*, the organ of the Central Committee of the Communist Party of Cuba, or in collections of works by Ernesto Che Guevara.

Four of the talks by Guevara are being published for the first time in English: the speech at the Central University of Las Villas; the March 1960 speech at the University of Havana; the farewell to the international volunteer work brigades; and the speech to the seminar on "Youth and the Revolution." Two others—the speech at the opening session of the First Latin American Youth Congress, and the talk to the International Meeting of Architecture Students—were published in English translation in the 1960s but have long been out of print. The remaining two—the talk to medical students and health workers, and the speech on the second anniversary of the unification of the youth organizations, appeared in *Che Guevara and the Cuban Revolution* published by Pathfinder Press in 1987.

The October 1997 speech by Cuban president Fidel Castro was published in *Granma*, and by the *Militant* newspaper in the United States.

~

A large team of volunteer translators gave generously of their time and abilities to assure the quality of the English-language edition. Pathfinder would like to express appreciation to Marty Anderson, Susan Apstein, Paul Coltrin, Robert Dees, Linda Joyce, Jennie Nilson, Aaron Ruby, and Matilde Zimmermann for their work. Final editing of the translations was the responsibility of Luis Madrid and Michael Taber.

Above: More than one million Cubans and international guests converge on Las Mercedes in the foothills of the Sierra Maestra mountains for July 26 celebration where Latin American Youth Congress was formally opened. **Below**: Congress participants join mass rally in Havana, August 7, 1960, where government decree nationalizing U.S.-owned corporations was approved by acclamation.

"When the Cuban Revolution speaks, it may make a mistake, but it will never tell a lie."

Something new in the Americas

To opening session of
First Latin American Youth Congress

July 28, 1960

Inspired by the example of the Cuban Revolution, which had brought down the U.S.-backed dictatorship of Fulgencio Batista a year and a half earlier and established a government that defended the interests of Cuba's workers and peasants, some nine hundred young people converged in Havana during the summer of 1960 to take part in the First Latin American Youth Congress. Delegates and observers attended from youth, labor, political, and solidarity organizations from every Latin American nation, as well as a number from the United States, Canada, the Soviet Union, China, and many other countries.

The formal opening of the congress in the Sierra Maestra mountains on July 26 was part of the national celebration of the seventh anniversary of the attack led by Fidel Castro on the dictatorship's Moncada and Bayamo garrisons. That audacious action in 1953 marked the beginning of the revolutionary struggle against the Batista regime. Participants in the two-week-long youth gathering reconvened in Havana on July 28, and Ernesto Che Guevara addressed its first plenary session.

The congress took place at a decisive turning point for the revolution.

Washington's hostility toward the actions taken by the workers and peasants of Cuba had been mounting sharply since May 1959, when the revolutionary government enacted one of the central planks of the program put forward by Fidel Castro during his trial for the Moncada attack: agrarian reform.

The law, implemented by the peasants and agricultural workers, who mobilized in support of the government decree, expropriated the vast plantations owned by U.S. corporations and big Cuban landlords. It gave title to the land, free of charge, to 100,000 tenant farmers, sharecroppers, and squatters, and created cooperative farms that provided stable year-round employment to hundreds of thousands of agricultural workers.

Although Washington showed no interest in discussing with Cuba any formula for payment, the law also provided for the indemnification of U.S. landowners by Cuban state bonds, payable in twenty years out of proceeds from the sale of Cuban sugar in the United States.

In June 1960, three major imperialist-owned oil trusts in Cuba announced their refusal to refine petroleum bought from the Soviet Union. The Cuban government responded by taking control of refineries owned by Texaco, Standard Oil, and Shell. U.S. president Dwight D. Eisenhower then ordered a drastic, 95 percent reduction in the quota of sugar Washington had earlier agreed to purchase from Cuba. Across the island, Cubans responded by proclaiming "Sin cuota pero sin bota"—without a quota but without the boot.

Youth congress participants were among those who took part in a mass rally in the wee hours of the morning August 7, where Fidel Castro read the revolutionary government's just-adopted decree expropriating the "assets and enterprises located on national territory . . . that are the property of U.S. legal entities." The following days and nights became known in Cuba as the Week of National Jubilation. Tens of thousands of Cubans, joined by many youth attending the congress, celebrated by marching through the streets of Havana bearing coffins containing the symbolic remains of U.S. enterprises, such as the United Fruit Company, International Telephone and Telegraph, and Standard Oil, and tossing them into the sea.

Over the next three months, Cuban workers and peasants mobilized in the millions, supported and organized by their new government, to defend their revolution. They occupied factories and fields and strengthened their volunteer militias. By late October virtually all imperialist-owned banks and industry, as well as the largest holdings of Cuba's capitalist class, had been expropriated by the workers and farmers government. They had become the property of Cuba. This transformation of property relations in city and countryside opened the first socialist revolution in the Americas.

Delegates to the Latin American Youth Congress worked in three commissions through August 8. They discussed and adopted resolutions, among others, extending their support to revolutionary Cuba, calling for international solidarity against Yankee imperialism, backing admission of the People's Republic of China to the United Nations, and demanding an end to racist discrimination and the creation of jobs and economic opportunities for youth throughout the Americas.

~

Compañeros of the Americas and the entire world:

It would take a long time to extend individual greetings on behalf of our country to each of you, and to each of the countries represented here. We nevertheless want to draw attention to some of those who are representing countries afflicted by natural catastrophes or catastrophes caused by imperialism.

We would like to extend special greetings tonight to the representative of the people of Chile, Clotario Blest, [*applause*] whose youthful voice you heard a moment ago.[1] Nevertheless, his maturity can serve as an example and a guide to our fellow working people from that unfortunate land, which has been devastated by one of the most terrible earthquakes in history.[2]

We would also like to extend special greetings to Jacobo Arbenz, [*applause*] president of the first Latin American nation [Guatemala] to fearlessly raise its voice against colonialism, and to express the cherished desires of its peasant masses through a deep-going and courageous agrarian reform. We would like to express our gratitude to him and to the democracy that fell in that country for the example it gave us, and for enabling us to make a correct appreciation of all the weaknesses that government was unable to overcome.[3] Doing so has made it possible for us to get to the root of the matter, and to decapitate in one blow those who held power, and the henchmen serving them.

We would also like to greet two of the delegations representing the countries that have perhaps suffered the most in the Americas. First of all, Puerto Rico, [*applause*] which even today, 150 years after freedom was proclaimed for the

---

1. Many of the names and events referred to in these speeches are identified in the glossary notes at the back of the book.

2. A series of earthquakes and tidal waves hit southern Chile May 21–29, killing more than 5,000 people.

3. See glossary notes, Guatemala coup, 1954.

first time in the Americas, continues fighting to take the first—and perhaps most difficult—step of achieving, at least formally, a free government. And I would like the delegates of Puerto Rico to convey my greetings, and those of all Cuba, to Pedro Albizu Campos. [*Applause*] We would like you to convey to Pedro Albizu Campos our deep-felt respect, our recognition of the example he has shown with his valor, and our fraternal feelings as free men toward a man who is free, despite being in the dungeons of the so-called U.S. democracy. [*Shouts of "Get rid of it!"*]

Although it may seem paradoxical, I would also like to greet today the delegation representing the purest of the North American people. [*Ovation*] I would like to salute them not only because the North American people are not to blame for the barbarity and injustice of their rulers, but also because they are innocent victims of the rage of all the peoples of the world, who sometimes confuse a social system with a people.

I therefore extend my personal greetings to the distinguished individuals I've named, and to the delegations of the fraternal peoples I've named. All of Cuba, myself included, open our arms to receive you and to show you what is good here and what is bad, what has been achieved and what has yet to be achieved, the road traveled and the road ahead. Because even though all of you come to deliberate at this Latin American Youth Congress on behalf of your respective countries, I'm sure each one of you came here full of curiosity to find out exactly what is this phenomenon born on a Caribbean island that is called the Cuban Revolution.

Many of you, from diverse political tendencies, will ask yourselves, as you did yesterday and as perhaps you will also do tomorrow: What is the Cuban Revolution? What is its ideology? And immediately a question will arise, as it always does in these cases, among both adherents and adversaries: Is the Cuban Revolution communist? Some say yes, hoping the answer is yes, or that it is heading in that direction. Others, disappointed perhaps, will also think the answer is yes. There will be those disappointed people who think the answer is no, as well as those who hope the answer is no.

I might be asked whether this revolution before your eyes is a communist revolution. After the usual explanations as to what communism is (I leave aside the hackneyed accusations by imperialism and the colonial powers, who confuse everything), I would answer that if this revolution is Marxist—and listen well that I say "Marxist"—it is because it discovered, by its own methods, the road pointed out by Marx. [*Applause*]

Recently, in toasting the Cuban Revolution, one of the leading figures of the Soviet Union, Vice Premier [Anastas] Mikoyan, [*applause*] a lifelong Marxist, said that it was a phenomenon Marx had not foreseen. [*Applause*] He then noted that life teaches more than the wisest books and the most profound thinkers. [*Applause*]

The Cuban Revolution was moving forward, not worrying about labels, not checking what others said about it, but constantly scrutinizing what the Cuban people wanted of it. And it quickly found that not only had it achieved, or was on the way to achieving, the happiness of its people; it had also become the object of inquisitive looks from friend and foe alike—hopeful looks from an entire continent, and furious looks from the king of monopolies.

But all this did not come about overnight. Permit me to relate some of my own experience—an experience that can help many people in similar circumstances get an understanding of how our current revolutionary thinking arose. Because even though there is certainly continuity, the Cuban Revolution you see today is not the Cuban Revolution of yesterday, even after the victory. Much less is it the Cuban insurrection prior to the victory, at the time when those eighty-two youths made the difficult crossing of the Gulf of Mexico in a leaky boat, to reach the shores of the Sierra Maestra.[4] Between those youths and the representatives of Cuba today there is a distance that cannot be measured in years—or at least not accurately measured in years, with twenty-four-hour days and sixty-minute hours.

All the members of the Cuban government—young in age, young in character, and young in the illusions they held—have nevertheless matured in the extraordinary school of experience; in living contact with the people, with their needs and aspirations.

The hope all of us had was to arrive one day somewhere in Cuba, and after a few shouts, a few heroic actions, a few deaths, and a few radio broadcasts, to take power and drive out the dictator Batista. History showed us it was much more difficult to overthrow a whole government backed by an army of murderers—murderers who were partners of that government and were backed by the greatest colonial power on earth.

That was how, little by little, all our ideas changed. We, the children of the cities, learned to respect the peasant. We learned to respect his sense of independence, his loyalty; to recognize his age-old yearning for the land that had been snatched from him; and to recognize his experience in the thousand paths through the hills. And from us, the peasants learned how valuable a man is when he has a rifle in his hand, and when he is prepared to fire that rifle at another man, regardless of how many rifles the other man has. The peasants taught us their know-how and we

---

4. See glossary notes, *Granma*.

taught the peasants our sense of rebellion. And from that moment until today, and forever, the peasants of Cuba and the rebel forces of Cuba—today the Cuban revolutionary government—have marched united as one.

The revolution continued progressing, and we drove the troops of the dictatorship from the steep slopes of the Sierra Maestra. We then came face-to-face with another reality of Cuba: the worker—both agricultural and in the industrial centers. We learned from him too; while we taught him that at the right moment, a well-aimed shot fired at the right person is much more powerful and effective than the most powerful and effective peaceful demonstration. [*Applause*] We learned the value of organization, while again we taught the value of rebellion. And out of this, organized rebellion arose throughout the entire territory of Cuba.

By then much time had passed. Many deaths marked the road of our victory—many in combat, others innocent victims. The imperialist forces began to see there was something more than a group of bandits in the heights of the Sierra Maestra, something more than a group of ambitious assailants arrayed against the ruling power. The imperialists generously offered their bombs, their bullets, their planes, and their tanks to the dictatorship. And with those tanks in the lead, the government's forces again attempted, for the last time, to ascend the Sierra Maestra.

By then, columns of our forces had already left the Sierra to invade other regions of Cuba and had formed the "Frank País" Second Eastern Front under Commander Raúl Castro.[5] [*Applause*] By then, our strength was growing within public opinion—we were now headline material in the international sections of newspapers in every corner

---

5. Formed in March 1958, the Rebel Army's Second Eastern Front was named after Frank País (see glossary notes)

of the world. Yet despite all this, the Cuban Revolution at that time possessed only 200 rifles—not 200 men, but 200 rifles—to stop the regime's last offensive, in which the dictatorship amassed 10,000 soldiers and every type of instrument of death.[6] The history of each one of those 200 rifles is a history of sacrifice and blood; they were rifles of imperialism that the blood and determination of our martyrs had dignified and transformed into rifles of the people. This was how the last stage of the army's great offensive unfolded, under the name of "encirclement and annihilation."

What I am saying to you, young people from throughout the Americas who are diligent and eager to learn, is that if today we are putting into practice what is called Marxism, it is because we discovered it here. In those days, after defeating the dictatorship's troops and inflicting 1,000 casualties on their ranks—that is, five times as many casualties as the sum total of our combat forces—and after seizing more than 600 weapons, a small pamphlet written by Mao Zedong fell into our hands. [*Applause*] That pamphlet, which dealt with the strategic problems of the revolutionary war in China, described the campaigns that Chiang Kai-shek carried out against the popular forces, which the dictator, just like here, called "campaigns of encirclement and annihilation."

Not only had the same words been used on opposite sides of the globe to designate their campaigns, but both dictators resorted to the same type of campaign to try to

---

6. In May 1958, the Batista regime launched an offensive to "encircle and annihilate" the Rebel Army in the Sierra Maestra. Despite the massive disparity in numbers of troops and scope and weight of equipment, the Batista army was defeated in numerous skirmishes. After a decisive battle at El Jigüe in mid-July, the troops of the tyranny withdrew, enabling the Rebel Army to assume the offensive throughout the island.

destroy the popular forces. And the popular forces here, without knowing the manuals that had already been written about the strategy and tactics of guerrilla warfare, used the same methods as those used on the opposite side of the world to combat the dictatorship's forces. Because naturally, whenever somebody goes through an experience, it can be utilized by somebody else. But it is also possible to go through the same experience without knowing of the earlier one.

We were unaware of the experiences the Chinese troops accumulated during twenty years of struggle in their territory. But we knew our own territory, we knew our enemy, and we used something every man has on his shoulders—which, if he knows how to use it, is worth a lot—we used our heads to guide our fight against the enemy. As a result, we defeated him.

Later came the westward invasions,[7] the breaking of Batista's communication lines, and the crushing fall of the dictatorship when no one expected it. Then came January 1, and the revolution—again without thinking about what it had read, but hearing what it needed to from the lips of the people—decided first and foremost to punish the guilty ones, and it did so.[8]

The colonial powers immediately splashed the story all over the front pages, calling it murder, and they immedi-

---

7. In late 1958 Guevara and Camilo Cienfuegos led Rebel Army columns west from the Sierra Maestra to Las Villas province in central Cuba. In a series of battles, the Batista forces were driven out of the major cities of the province, culminating in the capture of Santa Clara by Guevara's column on January 1, 1959, as Batista fled the country.

8. In the first weeks after the victory of the revolution, several hundred of the most notorious torturers and murderers of the Batista regime were executed. This measure had the overwhelming support of the Cuban people.

ately tried to do what the imperialists always try to do: sow division. "Communist murderers are killing people," they said, "but there is a naive patriot named Fidel Castro who had nothing to do with it and can be saved." [*Applause*] Using pretexts and trivial arguments, they tried to sow divisions among men who had fought for the same cause. They maintained this hope for some time.

But one day they came upon the fact that the Agrarian Reform Law approved here was much more violent and deep-going than the one their very brainy, self-appointed advisers had counseled.[9] All of them, by the way, are today in Miami or some other U.S. city. Pepín Rivero of *Diario de la Marina,* or Medrano of *Prensa Libre.* [*Shouts and hisses*] And there were others, including a prime minister in our government, who counseled great moderation, because "one must handle such things with moderation."[10]

"Moderation" is another one of the words colonial agents like to use. All those who are afraid, or who think of betraying in one way or another are moderates. [*Applause*] As for the people, in no sense are they moderates.

The advice given was to divide up marabú land—marabú is a wild shrub that plagues our fields—and have the peasants cut marabú with machetes, or settle in some

---

9. See glossary notes, Agrarian Reform Law.

10. José Miró Cardona. The first government that came to power in January 1959 included both revolutionary forces led by the July 26 Movement and bourgeois opposition figures. Among the latter were the new prime minister, José Miró Cardona, who was replaced as prime minister by Fidel Castro in February 1959; and Manuel Urrutia, who was president from January 1959 until July of that year, when he resigned under mounting popular pressure and was replaced by Osvaldo Dorticós of the July 26 Movement. From January 1 on, the Rebel Army, with Fidel Castro its commander in chief, was the sole, unchallenged, and increasingly popular armed force within Cuba.

swamp, or grab a piece of public land that somehow might have escaped the voraciousness of the large landowners. But to touch the holdings of the large landowners—that was a sin greater than anything they ever imagined to be possible. But it *was* possible.

I recall a conversation I had in those days with a gentleman who told me he had no problems at all with the revolutionary government, because he owned no more than nine hundred *caballerías*. Nine hundred caballerías comes to more than ten thousand hectares [25,000 acres].[11]

Of course, this gentleman did have problems with the revolutionary government; his lands were seized, divided up, and turned over to individual peasants. In addition, cooperatives were created on lands that agricultural workers were already becoming accustomed to working in common for a wage.

Here lies one of the peculiar features of the Cuban Revolution that must be studied. For the first time in Latin America, this revolution carried out an agrarian reform that attacked property relations other than feudal ones. There were feudal remnants in tobacco and coffee, and in these areas land was turned over to individuals who had been working small plots and wanted their land. But given how sugarcane, rice, and cattle were worked in Cuba, the land involved was seized as a unit and worked as a unit by workers who were given joint ownership. They are not owners of a single parcel of land, but of the whole great joint enterprise called a cooperative. This has enabled our deep-going agrarian reform to move rapidly. Each of you should let it sink in, as an incontrovertible truth, that no government here in Latin America can call itself revo-

---

11. One hectare equals 2.47 acres; in Cuba, one caballería equals 33 acres.

lutionary unless its first measure is an agrarian reform. [*Applause*]

Furthermore, a government that says it's going to implement a timid agrarian reform cannot call itself revolutionary. A revolutionary government is one that carries out an agrarian reform that transforms the system of property relations on the land—not just giving the peasants land that was not in use, but primarily giving the peasants land that *was* in use, land that belonged to the large landowners, the best land, with the greatest yield, land that moreover had been stolen from the peasants in past epochs. [*Applause*]

That is agrarian reform, and that is how all revolutionary governments must begin. On the basis of an agrarian reform the great battle for the industrialization of a country can be waged, a battle that is not so simple, that is very complicated, and where one must fight against very big things. We could very easily fail, as in the past, if it weren't for the existence today of very great forces in the world that are friends of small nations like ours. [*Applause*]

One must note here for the benefit of everyone—both those who like it and those who hate it—that at the present time countries such as Cuba, revolutionary countries, nonmoderate countries, cannot give a halfhearted answer to whether the Soviet Union or People's China is our friend. With all their might they must respond that the Soviet Union, China, and all the socialist countries, and many colonial or semicolonial countries that have freed themselves, are our friends. [*Applause*]

This friendship, the friendship with these governments throughout the world, is what makes it possible to carry out a revolution in Latin America. Because when they carried out aggression against us using sugar and petroleum, the Soviet Union was there to give us petroleum and buy sugar from us. Had it not been for that, we would have needed all our strength, all our faith, and all the devotion of this people—which is enormous—to withstand the blow this would have signified.[12] The forces of disunity would then have done their work, playing on the effects these measures taken by the "U.S. democracy" against this "threat to the free world" would have had on the living standards of the Cuban people. [*Applause*] They went after us viciously.

There are government leaders here in Latin America who still advise us to lick the hand that wants to hit us, and spit on the one that wants to help us. [*Applause*] We answer these government leaders who, in the middle of the twentieth century, recommend bowing our heads. We say, first of all, that Cuba does not bow down before anyone. And secondly, that Cuba, from its own experience, knows the weaknesses and defects of the governments that advise this approach—and the rulers of these countries know it too; they know it very well. Nevertheless, Cuba until now has not deigned or allowed itself, nor thought it permissible, to advise the rulers of these countries to shoot every traitorous official and nationalize all the monopoly holdings in their countries. [*Applause*]

The people of Cuba shot their murderers and dissolved the army of the dictatorship. Yet it has not been telling any government in Latin America to put the murderers of the people before the firing squad or to stop propping up dictatorships. But Cuba knows well there are murderers in each one of these nations. We can attest to that fact on the basis of a Cuban belonging to our own movement,

---

12. Following the U.S. government's July 3 decision to virtually end importation of sugar from Cuba, the Soviet Union announced it would purchase all Cuban sugar Washington refused to buy.

who was killed in a friendly country by henchmen left over from the previous dictatorship.[13] [*Applause and shouts of "To the wall!"*]

We do not ask that they put the person who assassinated one of our members before a firing squad, although we would have done so in this country. [*Applause*] What we ask, simply, is that if it is not possible to act with solidarity in the Americas, at least don't be a traitor to the Americas. Let no one in the Americas parrot the notion that we are bound to a continental alliance that includes our great enslaver, because that is the most cowardly and denigrating lie a ruler in Latin America can utter. [*Applause and shouts of: "Cuba sí, Yanquis no!"*]

We, who belong to the Cuban Revolution—who are the entire people of Cuba—call our friends friends, and our enemies enemies. We don't allow halfway terms: someone's either a friend or an enemy. [*Applause*] We, the people of Cuba, don't tell any nation on earth what they should do with the International Monetary Fund, for example. But we will not tolerate them coming to tell us what to do. We know what has to be done. If they want to do what we'd do, good; if not, that's up to them. But we will not tolerate anyone telling us what to do. Because we were here on our own up to the last moment, awaiting the direct aggression of the mightiest power in the capitalist world, and we did not ask help from anyone. We were prepared, together with our people, to resist up to the final consequences of our rebel spirit.

---

13. Andrés Coba, coordinator of the July 26 Movement in Venezuela—which organized solidarity with the Cuban Revolution—was gunned down July 27, 1960, in Caracas. The assailants were thought to be agents of Venezuela's political police. Coba died the morning of Guevara's speech.

That is why we can speak with our head held high, and with a very clear voice, in all the congresses and councils where our brothers of the world meet. When the Cuban Revolution speaks, it may make a mistake, but it will never tell a lie. From every tribune from which it speaks, the Cuban Revolution expresses the truth that its sons and daughters have learned, and it always does so openly to its friends and its enemies alike. It never throws stones from around a corner, nor gives advice that contains within it a dagger cloaked in velvet.

We are subject to attacks. We are attacked a great deal because of what we are. But we are attacked much, much more because we show to each nation of the Americas what it's possible to be. What's important for imperialism—much more than Cuba's nickel mines or sugar mills, or Venezuela's oil, or Mexico's cotton, or Chile's copper, or Argentina's cattle, or Paraguay's grasslands, or Brazil's coffee—is the totality of these raw materials upon which the monopolies feed.

That's why they put obstacles in our path every chance they get. And when they themselves are unable to erect obstacles, others in Latin America, unfortunately, are willing to do so. [*Shouts*] Names are not important, because no single individual is to blame. We cannot say that [Venezuelan] President Betancourt is to blame for the death of our compatriot and cothinker. President Betancourt is not to blame; President Betancourt is simply a prisoner of a regime that calls itself democratic. [*Shouts and applause*] That democratic regime, a regime that could have set another example in Latin America, nevertheless committed the great blunder of not using the firing squad in a timely way. So today the democratic government of Venezuela is a prisoner of the henchmen Venezuela was familiar with until a short while ago—and with whom Cuba was familiar, and the majority of Latin America remains familiar.

We cannot blame President Betancourt for this death. We can only say the following, backed by our record as revolutionaries, and by our conviction as revolutionaries: the day President Betancourt, elected by his people, feels himself a prisoner to such a degree that he cannot go forward and decides to ask the help of a fraternal people, Cuba is here to show Venezuela some of our experiences in the field of revolution. [*Applause*]

President Betancourt should know that it was not—and could not have been—our diplomatic representative who started this whole affair that ended in a death. It was they—the North Americans or the North American government in the final analysis; a bit closer, it was Batista's men. Closer still, it was all those dressed up in anti-Batista clothing who were the reserve forces of the U.S. government in this country—those who wanted to defeat Batista and maintain the system: people like [José] Miró Cardona, [Miguel Angel] Quevedo, [Pedro Luis] Díaz Lanz, and Huber Matos. [*Shouts*] And in direct line of sight, it was the forces of reaction operating in Venezuela. It is very sad to say, but the leader of Venezuela is at the mercy of his own troops, who may try to assassinate him, as happened a while ago with a car packed with dynamite.[14] The Venezuelan president, at this moment, is a prisoner of his repressive forces.

And this hurts. It hurts, because the Cuban people received from Venezuela the greatest amount of solidarity and support when we were in the Sierra Maestra. It hurts, because much earlier than us, Venezuela was at least able

---

14. On June 24, 1960, an attempt was made on the life of Venezuelan president Rómulo Betancourt when a car loaded with dynamite was detonated alongside his passing vehicle; he was unhurt.

to rid itself of the hateful system of oppression represented by [Marcos] Pérez Jiménez.

And it hurts, because when our delegation was in Venezuela—first Fidel Castro, and later our president Dorticós [*applause*]—they received the greatest demonstrations of support and affection.

A people who have achieved the high degree of political consciousness, who have the high fighting spirit of the Venezuelan people, will not long remain prisoners of a few bayonets or a few bullets. Because bullets and bayonets can change hands, and the murderers themselves can wind up dead.

But it is not my mission here to list all the stabs in the back we've received from Latin American governments in recent days and to add fuel to the fire of rebellion. That is not my task because, in the first place, Cuba is still not free of danger, and today it is still the focus of the imperialists' attention in this part of the world. Cuba needs the solidarity of all of you, the solidarity of those from the Democratic Action party in Venezuela, the URD [Democratic Republican Union], or the Communists, or COPEI [Independent Political Electoral Committee], or any other party. It needs the solidarity of all the people of Mexico, all the people of Colombia, Brazil, and each of the nations of Latin America.

It's true the colonialists are scared. They too, like everyone else, are afraid of missiles, they too are afraid of bombs. [*Applause*] And today they see, for the first time in their history, that these bombs of destruction can fall on their wives and children, on everything they had built with so much love—insofar as anyone can love wealth and riches. They began to make estimates; they put their electronic calculators to work, and they saw this setup would be self-defeating.

But this does not mean at all that they have renounced the suppression of Cuban democracy. They are again making laborious estimates on their calculating machines as to which of the alternative methods is best for attacking the Cuban Revolution. They have the Ydígoras method, the Nicaraguan method, the Haitian method. For the moment, they no longer have the Dominican method.[15] They also have the method of the mercenaries in Florida, the method of the OAS [Organization of American States]; they have many methods. And they have power; they have power to continue improving these methods.

President Arbenz and his people know they have many methods, and a great deal of might. Unfortunately for Guatemala, President Arbenz had an army of the old style, and was not fully aware of the solidarity of the peoples and their capacity to repel aggression of any type.

That is one of our greatest strengths: the strength being exerted throughout the world—regardless of partisan differences in any country—to defend the Cuban Revolution at any given moment. And permit me to say this is a duty of the youth of Latin America. Because what we have here in Cuba is something new, and it's something worth studying. I do not want to tell you what is good here; you will have to assess that yourselves.

There are many bad things, I know. There is much disorganization, I know. If you have been to the Sierra Maestra,

---

15. Gen. Miguel Ydígoras was military strongman in Guatemala from 1958 until 1963. The Somoza family dictatorship in Nicaragua lasted from 1933 to 1979. François (Papa Doc) Duvalier ruled Haiti from 1957 to 1971; he was succeeded by his son Jean-Claude (Baby Doc) Duvalier, who ruled until being overthrown in 1986. Rafael Leónidas Trujillo became dictator of the Dominican Republic in 1930. At the time Guevara gave this speech, Trujillo had lost Washington's favor; he was assassinated in 1961.

then you already know this. We still use guerrilla methods, I know. We lack technicians in fabulous quantities commensurate to our aspirations, I know. Our army has still not reached the necessary degree of maturity nor have the militia members achieved sufficient coordination to constitute themselves as an army, I know.

But what I also know—and what I want all of you to know—is that this revolution has always acted with the will of the entire people of Cuba. Every peasant and every worker, if they handle a rifle poorly, are working to handle it better every day, to defend *their* revolution. And if right now they can't understand the complicated workings of a machine whose technician fled to the United States, then they are studying every day to learn it, so *their* factory runs better. And the peasants will study *their* tractor, to fix its mechanical problems, so the fields of *their* cooperative yield more.

All Cubans, from both city and countryside, sharing the same sentiments, are marching toward the future, totally united in their thinking, led by a leader in whom they have absolute confidence, because he has shown in a thousand battles [*applause*] and on a thousand different occasions his capacity for sacrifice, and the power and foresight of his thought.

The nation before you today might disappear from the face of the earth because an atomic conflict may be unleashed on its account, and we might be the first target. Even if this entire island were to disappear along with its inhabitants, its people would consider themselves completely satisfied and fulfilled if each of you, upon returning to your countries, would say:

"Here we are. Our words come from the humid air of the Cuban forests. We have climbed the Sierra Maestra and seen the dawn, and our minds and our hands are filled with the seeds of that dawn. We are prepared to plant them in this land, and defend them so they can grow."

From all the brother countries of the Americas, and from our own land—if it should still remain standing as an example—from that moment on and forever, the voice of the peoples will answer: "Thus it shall be: Let freedom triumph in every corner of the Americas!" [*Ovation*]

Presiding over meeting of medical students in Havana, August 19, 1960, were, (right to left, in front row) medical doctors and commanders of the Rebel Army Oscar Fernández Mell, Che Guevara, and Minister of Public Health José Ramón Machado Ventura. Cuban poet Nicolás Guillén is at left.

"Training and nourishing the children, educating the army, distributing the lands of the absentee landlords among those who sweated every day on that same land without reaping its fruit — these tasks of the revolution constitute the greatest works of social medicine Cuba has achieved."

To be a revolutionary doctor you must first make a revolution

To medical students and health workers
August 19, 1960

The following speech by Che Guevara inaugurated a series of political talks and discussions organized by Cuba's Ministry of Public Health. The gathering was opened by José Ramón Machado, head of the ministry and, like Guevara, a doctor and a Rebel Army combatant whose courage and leadership had earned him the rank of commander. Held in the assembly hall of the Confederation of Cuban Workers (CTC), the gathering was attended by several hundred medical students and health workers, including militia members from the ministry. Representatives from throughout the continent taking part in the twelfth meeting of the Pan-American Health Organization, held in Havana August 14–26, were also present.

Following the August 6 decree expropriating the property of major U.S. corporations in Cuba, Washington and its client regimes in Latin America increased political and diplomatic pressure, as they accelerated military preparations, in hopes of stemming the revolutionary process and smothering Cuba's example. The foreign ministers of the Organization of American States met in Costa Rica August 16–28. As workers and youth demonstrated in solidarity with the Cuban Revolution in the streets of the capital, the ministerial gathering issued the Declaration of San José, denouncing Cuba for accepting aid from the Soviet Union and China. Cuban toilers and their revolutionary government responded to this assault on their national sovereignty at a September 2 rally of more than one million in the Plaza of the Revolution where the First Declaration of Havana was approved by acclamation.

Condemning "the exploitation of man by man, and the exploitation of the underdeveloped countries by imperialist finance capital," the declaration proclaimed "the right of the peasants to the land; the right of the workers to the fruit of their labor; the right of children to education; . . . the right of nations to nationalize the imperialist monopolies, thereby recovering their national wealth and resources; the right of countries to engage freely in trade with all the peoples of the world; the right of nations to their full sovereignty; the right of the peoples to turn fortresses into schools, and to arm their workers, peasants, students, intellectuals, Blacks, Indians, women, young people, old people, and all the oppressed and exploited, so they themselves may defend their rights and their destiny."

At the time of this gathering, the Ministry of Public Health's priority was the creation of a network of rural hospitals and clinics, to extend health care to the majority of peasants who had had no access to regular services; prior to the revolution there was one rural hospital in the entire country, located in Oriente province. Other measures that followed were the nationalization of drug companies and a sharp increase in the number of students training to be doctors, nurses, and medical technicians. A system of free medical care was progressively introduced and by 1963 covered the entire country.

~

Compañeros:

This modest ceremony is only one among hundreds being held as the Cuban people celebrate day by day their freedom and the advance of all their revolutionary laws, their advance along the road to total independence. But I find it interesting nonetheless.

Almost everyone knows that a number of years ago I started out my career to be a doctor. And when I started, when I began to study medicine, the majority of the concepts I hold today as a revolutionary were absent from the storehouse of my ideals.

I wanted to succeed, as everybody wants to succeed. I dreamed of being a famous researcher. I dreamed of working tirelessly to achieve something that could really be put at the disposal of humanity, but that would be a personal triumph at the same time. I was, as we all are, a child of my environment.

Through special circumstances and perhaps also because of my character, after receiving my degree I began to travel through Latin America and got to know it intimately. Except for Haiti and the Dominican Republic, I have visited—to one degree or another—all the countries of Latin America. Given how I traveled, first as a student and afterward as a doctor, I began to come into close contact with poverty, with hunger, with disease, with the inability to cure a child due to lack of resources, with the numbness that hunger and unrelenting punishment cause until a point is reached where a parent losing a child becomes an accident of no importance, as is often the case among those classes in our Latin American homeland who have been dealt the heaviest blows. And I began to see there was something that seemed to me almost as important as being a famous researcher or making a substantial contribution to medical science: it was helping those people.

But I continued to be, as all of us always are, a child of my environment, and I wanted to help people through my personal efforts. I had already traveled a lot—I was then in Guatemala, the Guatemala of Arbenz—and I had begun to make some notes to guide the conduct of a revolutionary doctor. I began to look into what was needed for me to be a revolutionary doctor.

However, the aggression came, the aggression unleashed by the United Fruit Company, the State Department, [John] Foster Dulles—they're really all the same thing— and by the puppet they put in who was named Castillo Armas—*was* named![1] The aggression was successful, since the people were not yet at the level of maturity the Cuban people have reached today. So one fine day, I, like many others, took the road of exile, or at least I took the road of fleeing Guatemala, since that was not my homeland.

Then I realized a fundamental thing: to be a revolutionary doctor, or to be a revolutionary, there must first be a revolution. The isolated effort, the individual effort, the purity of ideals, the desire to sacrifice an entire lifetime to the noblest of ideals—all that is for naught if the effort is made alone, solitary, in some corner of Latin America, fighting against hostile governments and social condi-

---

1. At the mass rally two weeks earlier where Cuban prime minister Fidel Castro read out the decree nationalizing the properties of U.S.-owned corporations in Cuba, the crowd responded to the name of each corporation with chants of *"Se llamaba!"—Was* named! The phrase became a popular slogan of the revolution. Castillo Armas was assassinated in 1957.

tions that permit no progress. A revolution needs what we have in Cuba: an entire people who are mobilized, who have learned the use of arms and the practice of unity in combat, who know what a weapon is worth and what the people's unity is worth.

Then we get to the heart of the problem that today lies ahead of us. We already have the right and even the obligation to be, before anything else, a revolutionary doctor, that is, a person who puts the technical knowledge of his profession at the service of the revolution and of the people. Then we come back to the earlier questions: How does one do a job of social welfare effectively? How does one reconcile individual effort with the needs of society?

Once again we have to recall what each of our lives was like prior to the revolution—what each of us did and thought, as a doctor or in any other public health function. We must do so with profound critical enthusiasm. And we will conclude that almost everything we thought and felt in that past epoch should be filed away, and we should create a new type of human being. If each one of us is his own architect in doing so, then creating that new type of human being—who will be the representative of the new Cuba—will be much easier.

It is good for you—those present here, residents of Havana—to absorb this idea: that in Cuba a new type of human being is coming into existence, one that cannot be entirely appreciated in the capital, but that can be seen in every corner of the country. Those of you who went to the Sierra Maestra on July 26 must have seen two absolutely unheard-of things: an army with picks and shovels, one that takes such pride in marching in the patriotic celebrations in Oriente province with its picks and shovels ready, side by side with the militia compañeros marching with their rifles. [*Applause*] But you must also have seen something much more important: You must have seen some children who by their physical stature appear eight or nine years old, but who are nevertheless almost all thirteen or fourteen. They are the most authentic children of the Sierra Maestra, the most authentic children of hunger and poverty in all its forms. They are the creatures of malnutrition.

In this small Cuba, with four or five television channels, with hundreds of radio stations, despite all the advances of modern science, when those children for the first time came to school at night and saw electric lights, they exclaimed that the stars were very low that night. Those children, whom some of you would have seen, have now been brought together in schools where they are learning everything from the ABCs right up to a trade, right up to the very difficult science of being a revolutionary.

These are the new types of human beings emerging in Cuba. They are being born in isolated places, in remote points in the Sierra Maestra and also in the cooperatives and workplaces.

All that has a lot to do with the topic of our talk today: the integration of the doctor or any other medical worker into the revolutionary movement. Because the revolution's tasks—of training and nourishing the children, educating the army, distributing the lands of the absentee landlords among those who sweated every day on that same land without reaping its fruit—those are the greatest works of social medicine that Cuba has achieved.

The principle of creating a robust body should be the basis of the battle against disease—not creating a robust body through a doctor's artistic work on a weak organism, but creating a robust body through the work of the whole collectivity, especially the whole social collectivity.

Someday medicine will have to become a science that

serves to prevent disease, to orient the entire public toward their medical obligations, and that only in cases of emergency intervenes to perform some surgical operation, or to deal with something outside the characteristics of that new society we are creating.

The work entrusted today to the Ministry of Health, to all the institutions of this type, is to organize public health in such a way as to aid the greatest possible number of people, to prevent everything foreseeable related to disease, and to orient the people. But to carry out the organizational task, as for all revolutionary tasks, what is required, fundamentally, is the individual. The revolution is not, as some claim, a standardizer of collective will, of collective initiative. To the contrary, it is a liberator of the individual capacity of human beings.

What the revolution does do, however, is to orient that capacity. And our task today is to orient the creative talent of all the medical professionals toward the tasks of social medicine.

We are at the end of an era, and not only here in Cuba. Despite everything said to the contrary, and despite all the hopes of some people, the forms of capitalism we have known, under which we have been raised and have suffered, are being defeated throughout the world. [*Applause*]

The monopolies are being defeated. Every day science, the collective work of many, registers new and important triumphs. It is our proud and self-sacrificing duty to be the vanguard in Latin America of a liberation movement that began some time ago in the other subjugated continents of Africa and Asia. That very profound social change also demands profound changes in the mentality of the people.

Individualism as such, as the isolated action of a person alone in a social environment, must disappear in Cuba. Individualism tomorrow should be the proper utilization of the whole individual, to the absolute benefit of the community. But even when all this is understood today, even when these things I am saying are comprehended—and even when everyone is willing to think a little about the present, about the past, and about what the future should be—changing the way we think requires profound internal changes, and helps bring about profound external changes, primarily social.

Those external changes are taking place in Cuba every day. One way of learning about this revolution—of getting to know the forces the people have kept stored inside themselves, forces that have lain dormant for so long—is to visit the length and breadth of Cuba, visit the cooperatives and all the workplaces being created. And one way of getting to the heart of the medical question is not only knowing these places, not only visiting them, but also getting to know the people who make up those cooperatives and workplaces. Go and find out what diseases they have, what their ailments are, what extreme poverty they have lived in over the years, inherited from centuries of repression and total submission.

The doctor, the medical worker, should then go to the heart of his new work, that of a person among the masses, a person within the community.

Whatever happens in the world, the doctor—by always being close to the patient, by knowing his psyche so deeply, by representing those who live close to pain and alleviate it—has a very important job, one with great responsibility in society.

Some time ago, a few months, a group of students here in Havana, recently certified as doctors, did not want to go to the countryside and were demanding extra payment for doing so. From the viewpoint of the past, this was not out of the ordinary, at least it seems that way to me, and

I understand it perfectly. This was the way it was, the way I remember it being some years ago. It is the rebellious gladiator once again, the solitary fighter who wants to ensure a better future, better conditions, and to make others appreciate the necessity of what he does.

But what would happen if it were not those boys—the majority of whose families could afford several years of study—who completed their courses and were now beginning to practice their profession? What if instead 200 or 300 peasants had emerged, as if by magic, from the university lecture halls?

What would have happened, simply, is that those peasants would have run immediately, and with great enthusiasm, to attend to their brothers and sisters. They would have asked for the posts with the most responsibility and the hardest work, in order to show that the years of study they had been given were not in vain. What would have happened is what will happen within six or seven years, when the new students, children of the working class and the peasantry, receive their professional degrees of whatever type. [*Applause*]

But let's not approach the future with fatalism and divide people into children of the working class or peasantry and counterrevolutionaries. Because that is simplistic, because it is not true, and because there is nothing that educates an honorable man more than living within a revolution. [*Applause*]

None of us, none of the first group that arrived on the *Granma*, who established ourselves in the Sierra Maestra and learned to respect the peasant and the worker, living together with him—none of us had a past as a worker or peasant. Naturally, there were those who had had to work, who had known certain wants in their childhood. But hunger, true hunger—that none of us had known, and we began to know it, temporarily, during the two long years in the Sierra Maestra. And then many things became very clear.

We, who at the outset severely punished anyone who touched even an egg of some rich peasant or landowner, one day took ten thousand head of cattle to the Sierra and said to the peasants simply: "Eat." And the peasants, for the first time in many years—some for the first time in their lives—ate beef.

In the course of the armed struggle, the respect we had for the sacrosanct ownership of those ten thousand head of cattle was lost, and we understood perfectly that the life of a single human being is worth millions of times more than all the property of the richest man on earth. [Applause] And we learned it there, we who were not sons of the working class or the peasantry. So why should we shout to the four winds that now we are the superior ones and that the rest of the Cuban people cannot learn too? Yes, they can learn. In fact, the revolution today demands that they learn. It demands they understand that pride in serving our fellow man is much more important than a good income; that the people's gratitude is much more permanent, much more lasting than all the gold one can accumulate. [Applause] And each doctor, within the scope of his activity, can and should accumulate that prized treasure, the people's gratitude.

We must then begin to erase our old concepts and come ever closer to the people, and with an ever more critical spirit as we do so. Not in the way we got closer before, because all of you will say: "No, I am a friend of the people. I enjoy talking with workers and peasants, and on Sundays I go to such and such a place to see such and such a thing." Everybody has done that. But that is practicing charity, and what we have to practice today is solidarity.

[*Applause*] We should not draw closer to the people in order to say: "Here we are. We come to give you the charity of our presence, to teach you with our science, to demonstrate your errors, your lack of refinement, your lack of elementary knowledge." We should go with an investigative zeal and with a humble spirit, to learn from the great source of wisdom that is the people. [*Applause*]

Often we realize how mistaken we were in concepts that we took so much for granted that they had become part of us and, automatically, part of what we thought we knew. Often we should change all our concepts—not just general, social, or philosophical concepts, but also, at times, our medical concepts. We will see that diseases are not always treated as one treats an illness in a big-city hospital. We will see that the doctor also has to be a farmer, that he has to learn to cultivate new foods and, by his example, to cultivate the desire to consume new foods, to diversify the nutritional structure in Cuba—so meager and so poor in an agricultural country that is potentially the richest on earth. We will see that under these circumstances we have to be a little bit pedagogical, at times very pedagogical. We will see that we also have to be politicians; that the first thing we have to do is not to offer our wisdom, but to show we are ready to learn with the people, to carry out that great and beautiful common experience—to build a new Cuba.

We have already taken many steps, and the distance between January 1, 1959, and today cannot be measured in the conventional manner. Some time ago, the people understood that not only had a dictator fallen here, but a system as well. Now the people should learn that upon the ruins of a crumbled system, one must build a new one that brings about the people's absolute happiness.

I remember when Compañero [Nicolás] Guillén returned from Argentina early last year. He was the same great poet he is today—perhaps his books were translated into one fewer language, because every day he wins new readers in all the languages of the world, but he was the same as today. But it was difficult for Guillén to read his poems, which were poems of the people, because that was the first period, the period of prejudices. Nobody ever stopped to think that for years and years, with incorruptible dedication, the poet Guillén had put all his extraordinary artistic gifts at the service of the people and at the service of the cause he believed in. The people saw in him not the glory of Cuba, but the representative of a political party that was taboo. But all that is behind us. We have already learned that if we have a common enemy, and if we are trying to reach a common goal, then we cannot have divisions based on opinions about certain internal structures in our country. What we need to agree on is whether or not we have a common enemy, and whether or not we have a common goal. [*Applause*]

We all have definitively become convinced there is a common enemy. Today no one looks over their shoulder to see if someone might overhear them, if some embassy spy might report his opinions, before clearly speaking out against the monopolies, before clearly saying: "Our enemy, and the enemy of all Latin America, is the monopolistic government of the United States of America." [*Applause*]

If everybody already knows this is the enemy, and if our starting point is knowing that whoever struggles against that enemy has something in common with us, then the second part follows: What are our goals here in Cuba? What do we want? Do we want people to be happy or not? Are we struggling for Cuba's absolute economic liberation or not? Are we or are we not struggling to be a free country among free countries, without belonging to any military bloc, without having to consult any embassy of any great power on earth about domestic or foreign decisions we make? Are we thinking of redistributing the wealth of those who have too much, to give to those who have nothing? [*Applause*] Are we thinking here of making creative work a dynamic daily source of all our happiness? If so, then we already have the goals to which we referred. And everyone who shares those goals is our friend. If that person also has other ideas, if he belongs to one or another organization, those are discussions of lesser importance.

At times of great dangers, at times of great tensions and great creations, what counts are the great enemy and the great goals. If we agree, if all of us already know where we are going, then whatever happens, we must begin our work. [*Applause*]

I was telling you that to be a revolutionary you have to have a revolution. We already have it. And a revolutionary must also know the people with whom he is to work. I think we still don't know one another well. I think we still have to travel a while along that road. If someone asks me how to go about getting to know the people, in addition to going into the interior, learning about cooperatives, living in cooperatives (and not everybody can do that, and there are many places where the presence of a medical worker is very important) . . . in those cases, I will tell you that one of the Cuban people's greatest expressions of solidarity is the revolutionary militias. [*Applause*] The militias now give the doctor a new function and prepare him for what was at least until recently a sad and almost fatal reality in Cuba: that is, that we were going to be prey—or if not prey at least victims—of a large-scale armed attack.

I must caution that as a revolutionary militia member, a doctor must always be a doctor. He should not commit the error we made in the Sierra—or perhaps it was not an error, but all the doctor compañeros of that period know it's the case—that it seemed dishonorable to us to be at the side of someone wounded or ill, and we sought any means possible to grab a rifle and show on the battlefield what should be done.

Now conditions are different, and the new armies being formed to defend the country should be armies that use a different method. Within this new army the doctor will have enormous importance. He should continue being a doctor, which is one of the most beautiful and most important tasks of war. And not just the doctor but also the nurses, laboratory technicians, all those who dedicate themselves to this humane profession.

But even knowing that danger is present, and even while preparing to repel the aggression that still hangs over us— we should all stop thinking about it. Because if we center our efforts on war preparations, we cannot build what we want, we cannot devote ourselves to creative work.

All work, all capital invested in preparing for military action, is labor lost, money lost. Unfortunately, it has to be done, because others are preparing. But the money I am most saddened to see leave the National Bank coffers—and I say this with all honesty and pride as a soldier—is money to pay for some weapon of destruction. [*Applause*]

The militias have a function in peacetime, however. The militias should be, in the populated areas, the arm that unifies and gets to know the people. They should practice real solidarity, as the compañeros have told me is being done in the medical militias. At times of danger, they should immediately set out to resolve the problems of the needy throughout Cuba. But the militias are also an opportunity to get to know one another, an opportunity for the men of all Cuba's social classes to live side by side, made equal and made brothers by a common uniform.

If we medical workers achieve this—and you'll allow me to use once again this term I had forgotten some time ago—if we all use that new weapon of solidarity, if we know the goals, if we know the enemy, and if we know the direction in which we must travel, then the only thing left for us is to know the daily stretch of the road and to take it. Nobody can point out that stretch—it is the personal road of each individual; it is what he will do every day, what he will gain from his individual experience, and what he will give of himself in practicing his profession, dedicated to the people's well-being.

If we already possess all the elements with which to march toward the future, let us recall that phrase of Martí, which at this moment I am not putting into practice, but which we must constantly put into practice: "The best form of saying is doing." Let us then march toward the future of Cuba. [*Ovation*]

Volunteer work brigades of youth from around the world helped construct the Camilo Cienfuegos school complex in the Sierra Maestra, shown above. **Below**: Brigade members at farewell rally in Havana.

"Have the people of this country made a revolution because that's just the way they are? Absolutely not. The people are the way they are because they are in the midst of a revolution."

In Cuba imperialism was caught sleeping, but now it is awake

Farewell to international volunteer work brigades
September 30, 1960

The Cuban Revolution won the solidarity of working people and youth the world over. In August and September 1960 some 160 young people from 36 countries volunteered their labor for nearly two months to help build the "Camilo Cienfuegos" school complex in Las Mercedes in the Sierra Maestra mountains. Guevara gave the following speech at a ceremony bidding farewell to these volunteer work brigades.

The delegation from Algeria received special mention by Guevara. Since 1954 the National Liberation Front had been fighting an independence war against Paris that had become a pole of attraction for revolutionary-minded youth the world over. In 1962 the French colonial regime conceded defeat and Algeria, like Cuba, established a government, under the leadership of Ahmed Ben Bella, that mobilized workers and peasants to defend their own interests.

Four days prior to Guevara's speech, Fidel Castro had addressed the United Nations General Assembly for the first time, placing before the world the case for Cuba's right to national self-determination and economic development. "The case of Cuba is not an isolated one," Castro pointed out. It "is the case of all the underdeveloped and colonized countries." Speaking on behalf of Cuba's revolutionary government, Castro denounced the actions of the United Nations in giving cover to the U.S.-organized overthrow of the government of Patrice Lumumba in the Congo days earlier. He underscored Cuba's support for Algeria's independence struggle against France, called for UN recognition of the People's Republic of China, and solidarized with the struggle for Puerto Rico's freedom from U.S. colonial rule.

On September 28, 1960, at a mass rally in Havana, Fidel Castro reported back to the Cuban people on his historic trip to New York during which the entire delegation—made unwelcome at a downtown hotel—had moved uptown to the Hotel Theresa, receiving a tumultuous welcome from the people of Harlem and a warm embrace from U.S. revolutionary leader Malcolm X.

At that same mass gathering in Havana, during which a bomb planted by counterrevolutionary terrorists exploded, Castro announced that a block-by-block organization of Cubans mobilized against the counterrevolution would be created. In the coming days the Committees for the Defense of the Revolution would be organized to meet this necessity.

∼

Compañeros of Cuba and from all the countries of the world who took your message of solidarity with the Cuban Revolution to the foothills of the Sierra Maestra:

Today is a happy day, a youthful day, but it's also a sad day of farewell. Today we say "so long" to the compañeros who came here from all over the world to work for the Cuban Revolution, and to get to know this revolution and its people. You worked with all your youthful and revolutionary enthusiasm. I believe you also got to know our people, a people like any other, made up of millions of individuals who now form a unified and fighting mass in defense of their newly acquired rights—millions standing firm until death in order to safeguard those rights and continue advancing toward new conquests. [*Applause*]

It would be an error for us to presume to explain to each of the compañeros who have come from around the world what a revolution is. It would also be an error to try to get them to follow this example, as if it were something unique in the world. This is nothing more, but also nothing less, than a people who have taken the road of revolution, and they stand firmly on it. Many of the world's young people now know what it means to take the road of revolution, just as Cubans know. They know the magnificent results the people obtain when they cut themselves loose from the obstacles that hindered their development.

Unfortunately there are also many compañeros in the Americas and throughout the world who have not yet seen their people take the road of revolution. Perhaps they do not yet fully understand the historic phenomenon that allowed Cuba—a country no more colonized or exploited than any other—to find, in its desperation, the necessary strength to begin the struggle that would break its chains. In truth, from the standpoint of well-known theories, it is difficult to explain why it was precisely here in Cuba that the first battle cry for the definitive liberation of the Americas was sounded, and here that we continue advancing even now. We will not presume to explain it, either. We don't presume that the Cuban example is the only way to realize the aspirations of a people. Nor do we believe that this road paved with struggle is the one and only way to achieve true happiness, that is, freedom and economic well-being. Be that as it may, much of what we have done can be achieved in almost any oppressed country, whether oppressed, colonized, semicolonized. Not underdeveloped, as they call us, because we are not underdeveloped. We are simply badly developed, badly developed because imperialism long ago took over our raw materials and set out to exploit them according to its own imperial needs.

It is unnecessary to give a lot of examples. You know about Cuba's sugar, Mexico's cotton, Venezuela's oil, Bolivia's tin, Chile's copper, Argentina's cattle and wheat, or Brazil's coffee. We all share a common denominator: we are countries that produce a single product, and we also share the common denominator of being countries dependent on a single market.

We therefore know that on the road to liberation we must first struggle to free ourselves from the single market, and then from having only a single product to sell. Foreign trade and domestic production must also be diversified. Up to this point everything is very simple. The question is how to do it. By the parliamentary road? By way of arms? Or through a combination of the parliamentary road and the armed road? I don't know, and I can't respond accurately to the question. What I can tell you, however, is that under Cuba's conditions of oppression by imperialism and its local puppets, we saw no way out for the Cuban people other than the voice of guns.

To those bogged down by technicalities—who ask us, for example, how much capital do you need to begin an agrarian reform—we would say none; the only capital needed is that of an armed people conscious of their rights. [*Applause*] That was the only capital we needed here in Cuba to carry out our agrarian reform, to deepen it, to advance it, and to embark on the road of industrialization.

Of course, all the people's efforts cannot be summed

up in a simple formula, because this struggle has cost blood and suffering, and the world's empires are trying to make it cost more blood and suffering. That's why we must firmly unite around those rifles, around the only voice that guides the entire people toward their final goals. We must be firmly united, allowing nothing to sow division. Because if brothers quarrel—as Martín Fierro said—outsiders will devour them. And this maxim, which the poet simply got from the people, is one imperialism knows all too well: if you divide, you conquer. For that reason it divided us into countries that produce coffee, copper, oil, tin, or sugar. It divided us, too, into countries competing for the market of a single country, constantly lowering prices, so it could more easily defeat our countries one by one.

In other words, any rule that can be applied to one people has to be applied to all peoples whose development is incomplete. We must all be united. All the world's peoples should unite to get what is most sacred: freedom; economic well-being; the conviction that they will never face a problem that is insurmountable; and the knowledge that through our daily, enthusiastic, and creative labor we can achieve our goals and nothing can stop us.

But empires do exist, and you know them. We know them too because they have exploited us. The compañeros born inside these empires also know them, because they have lived in the belly of the beast, and they know how terrible it is to live under such conditions when one has faith in humanity. All peace-loving countries—encircled today by bases with nuclear weapons, unable to fulfill their aspirations of development—know them too.

We all know them, and for this reason our common duty is to try to unite despite the governments that want to keep us apart. We must clasp hands—not just with young people, as we did here, but also with older people, the elderly and the children—so we become a single will. We must clasp hands to avoid the most terrible of wars threatening humanity today, as well as to achieve everyone's most cherished desires.

As soon as the peoples, who are aware of all this—because they are not ignorant—want to achieve this unity, pressure begins to be exerted by all the countries with sell-out rulers. This will happen to many of you. They will throw you in jail, oppress you in any way possible. They will try to make you forget what you learned in a free country, or to make an example of you so the fainthearted have no desire to follow the road of dignity. This has already happened to many of those who visited us from countries in Latin America and, unfortunately, it will continue to occur. Many of you will run into problems. Many of you will be labeled human beings of the worst sort, allied with strange foreign oppressors, with the most vile elements, out to destroy what they call democracy, out to destroy the Western way of life.

Ask the struggling people of Algeria about their Western way of life. Or ask any of the peoples who fight and are killed every day for seeking a happiness that never seems to arrive.

That's why it is not an easy road, even for those like us who have overcome the first barrier, and established a government of the people. [*Applause*] A very difficult stage is still ahead, a stage when these false democracies will attack the people more and more, when the people's indignation and even hatred will well up inside them, until they form a human wave that takes up arms, fights, and conquers power. Under the conditions currently faced by humanity, peoples in the colonial and semicolonial countries—those under the yoke of the empires' puppet governments—will almost certainly have to take up arms sooner or later to be able to put their representatives in the government, and in this way unite all of America, all of Africa, all of Asia. Then America, Africa, Asia, and Europe will all be together in a single happy world. [*Applause*]

But you will see many things. You will see how in Cuba imperialism was caught sleeping but is now awake. The cries of the people woke it up. You will see them create police forces, which will be called international, where leadership will be assigned to those with more experience in the fight against communism. In other words, in the case of our Latin American example, it will be the United States that will take up arms to combat any people that rebels—or, more precisely, that will provide the arms that our brothers in the Americas will carry under the shameful flag of what is today the Organization of American States. This will be seen in the Americas, and soon. It will be seen because the peoples will rebel and because imperialism will create those armies. But the history of the world marches on, and we will see—or our compañeros will see, in the event we fall in the struggle, but in any case this generation will see—how in the struggle the peoples will defeat armies equipped by the most brutal power on earth, and they will destroy imperialism completely.

Our generation will see the world definitively liberated, [*applause*] even if we have to experience the greatest suffering, the greatest hardships, and even if in their madness they seek to unleash a war that will only hasten their demise.

But if any nation achieves its independence without having to pass through this struggle, or is able to shorten some of its stages, and asks us for the recipe to unify the people, to organize the deepest economic and social reforms using the capital of guns and the people—then we must tell them that it is very important to educate the people, and that the people can be educated with marvelous speed.

Those of us who have had the opportunity to live through an experience like the Cuban Revolution, so rich in events, are moved when we see how day by day our people gain more knowledge, more revolutionary conviction, more revolutionary consciousness. Take a simple example from today: All the delegations from brother countries were warmly applauded. But three of them received our warmest applause because they face special circumstances.

One is the delegation of the people of the United States of America, [*applause*] a delegation that should never be confused with the government of the United States of America. It is a delegation of people with no racial hatred, and who do not judge individuals by their skin color, their religion, or their economic status.

Also receiving very warm applause were those who today represent better than anyone the opposite pole, the delegation from the People's Republic of China. [*Applause*]

At the same time, two other peoples were applauded, from countries whose governments are in bitter struggle—one backed by its entire people, the other deceiving its people or against its people. So the Algerian delegation was also enthusiastically welcomed. [*Applause*] They are writing another marvelous page in history, fighting the way we had to in the mountains. But they are facing an invasion that did not originate on their own soil. People born on your own soil, however brutal they may be, always observe some semblance of respect. The Algerian people, however, face an invasion by troops of a foreign country, who are taught to slaughter, who are taught racial hatred, who are taught the philosophy of war. In spite of this our people were able to applaud, very generously, the delegation of the people of France, who also do not represent their government. [*Applause*]

Ours is a people who know how to choose so accurately the object of their applause, who know how to find the political essence of things, who know how to make such a precise distinction between peoples and governments, even in moments like this—when, for example, bitter hatred and brutal repression have been directed against the Cuban delegation in the United Nations, reaching the point of physical threats, not to mention verbal threats. So we ask ourselves: Have the people of this country made a revolution because that's just the way they are? Absolutely not. The people are the way they are because they are in the midst of a revolution. In the process of exercising their revolutionary rights during the barely twenty months of the Cuban Revolution, they have learned all that is being expressed here today and all that you, delegates from around the world, have been able to see and witness in our island.

The first prescription for educating the people, to put it in different words, is for them to take the road of revolution. Never try to teach a people that through education alone and under a despotic government, they can conquer their rights. Teach them, first and foremost, to conquer their rights. When they have a government that represents them, they will learn everything taught to them, and even more: they will themselves become teachers of everyone without the slightest effort. [*Applause*]

We ourselves, a revolutionary government, part of the people, have learned by always asking the people and without ever isolating ourselves from them. Because he who governs, yet isolates himself in an ivory tower and tries to lead the people with formulas, is lost and is on the road to despotism. The people and the government should always be one. And all of you, visiting compañeros of the Americas and of colonial countries that are yet to win their independence, should also be aware that to lead the people you do not need a lot of schooling. If you have it, good. If you are a philosopher or a mathematician, good. But to lead the people you have to interpret them. And that is much easier to do if you are part of them, if you have never let education, or any other barrier that separates us, isolate you from them.

That is why we have a government of workers, of peasants, and includes as well people who knew how to read from before. But the latter, who are a minority, learned a lot more in the struggle. And you have the example here, in the Rebel Youth. [*Applause*] On Sunday you will hear Commander Joel Iglesias. [*Applause*] This Rebel Army commander went to the Sierra when he was fifteen, barely able to read and not knowing how to write. Today he is able to address all the youth, not because he has become a philosopher in a year and a half, but because he speaks to the people as one of them, because he feels what all of you feel every day, and he knows how to express it, he knows how to reach you. If governments were made up of men like him, that would be better.

Therefore, we extend here our greetings to the governments of the world whose leaders have suffered as part of the people, who have learned their ABCs in the course of the struggle, and are today, as always, identified with the people. [*Applause*]

You have come here, compañeros of the world, to know us and to work for us. But in spite of all the knowledge you bring us, you can always learn something new, especially compañeros from countries that have not had this experience and are preparing for it. Because all this is part of history, and past history cannot be changed.

There are many things to learn from Cuba. Not only the

good things, which you see every day, those that show the enthusiasm and fervor of the people. You can also learn from the bad things, so that one day, when you have to govern, you can avoid the kind of errors we have committed. You can learn how organization must be intimately tied to the victory of the people, that the more thorough the organization, the easier the victory.

You set out to build a school complex, but when you arrived not everything was organized. The school complex was on break, and you were not able to finish that small monument to human solidarity that you wanted to leave there. That's a shame, although for us it's worth as much as if you had built the grandest castle. But it is also a lesson that organization is important. We cannot think that a revolutionary is a divine being who, by the grace of God, falls to earth, opens his arms, and the revolution begins. That when problems arise, they are resolved simply by the grace of the enlightened. A revolutionary must be a tireless worker, and more than tireless, organized. If instead of learning from the struggle's setbacks, as we have had to do, you go into the revolutionary struggle bringing with you that prior organizational experience, all the better for those countries where each of you will fight to make a revolution. This is one of the lessons you can take from here. And you can draw the lesson from this concrete example, since we could not offer you a positive one.

But, of course, in many other branches of the country's economy we have not committed this sin. From the early days of the struggle we learned that we had to organize ourselves. And even though the revolution is barely completing its second year, we are preparing our first well-organized development plan, to carry it out enthusiastically, along with the entire people. Because an ambitious development plan, which will seek to harness all the forces of the people, cannot be divorced from them. We must do it together, so that everyone understands it, so that everyone grasps its essence, and so that everyone puts their shoulder to the wheel for this task.

We will be the first country in the Americas that can say with pride that we have a plan for economic development and, moreover, we have the most important thing, a plan that will be fulfilled, a plan we will do everything possible to surpass. [*Applause*] Why do we need this plan? For us this is also something new; because we always have to think over carefully all those things we do not fully understand. We must analyze what the enemy wants us to do and why they want us to do it. Then we must do the opposite. The enemy doesn't want us to plan, to organize, to nationalize our economy; the enemy fights with all its might against it. Why? Because it is precisely through the capitalist anarchy of production that they exploit working people. That is how they make everyone develop a dog-eat-dog mentality, where each one struggles on his own, elbowing each other, kicking each other, knocking heads; each person trying to get ahead of everyone else, failing to realize that if we got organized and united we would be a tremendous force and could go much further, to the benefit of everyone. [*Applause*]

Of course, there are always individuals, at least a few, who watch the bullfight from behind the barrier, those who stay away from daily work and effort, who get offended by hearing these things, and who, aghast, speak of the sanctity of private property. What has private property meant, the property of the big monopolies? (We're not talking about the small workshop or store owner, but the big monopolies.) What it has meant is the destruction not only of our strengths but also of our national identity and our culture. The monopoly—which is the epitome of private property, the epitome of the struggle of man against man—is the imperial weapon that divides, that exploits, and that degrades the people. Monopolies produce cheaper goods, but these are either of poor quality or are not needed. They sell their culture through movies, novels, or children's stories, fully intent on instilling within us a different mentality. Because they have their strategy—the strategy of laissez-faire; the strategy of individual versus collective effort, of appealing to that little bit of selfishness that exists in each person to beat out the rest. They appeal to that petty superiority complex that everyone possesses that makes one think they are better than everybody else. The monopolies instill in individuals, from childhood on, the view that since you are better and work harder, that it is in your interest to struggle individually against everyone else, to defeat everyone else and become an exploiter yourself.

The monopolies go to great lengths to prove that collective effort enslaves and prevents the smarter and more capable from getting ahead. As if the people were made up simply of individuals, some more intelligent, some more capable. As if the people were something other than a great mass of wills and hearts that all have more or less the same capacity for work, the same spirit of sacrifice, and the same intelligence.

They go to the undifferentiated masses and try to sow divisions: between blacks and whites, more capable and less capable, literate and illiterate. They then subdivide people even more, until they single out the individual and make the individual the center of society.

The monopolies, needless to say, stand above these individuals they point to. Monopolies are collectivities, too, but they are collectivities of exploitation. We have to show people that their strength rests not in considering themselves better than everyone else, but in knowing their individual limitations as well as the strength of unity; in knowing that two can always push harder than one, ten more than two, a hundred more than ten, and six million more than a hundred! [*Applause*]

Compañeros, delegates from around the world: I must thank you, on behalf of the Cuban people, and tell you sincerely that we have learned a lot from you, and that you leave an indelible mark on us. But we also hope we have left an indelible mark on you. We hope you take advantage of all we have to offer. We hope that wherever in the world it becomes necessary to analyze why things are the way they are, that you do so; that you study the theories, revise them, and analyze them carefully. And we hope that everyone will ask themselves whether it is possible to be happy some day, and what will be the means to bring that about.

We do not presume to put ourselves forward as an example. We simply offer this, with open arms, as a historical fact. If someone can draw lessons from us that are of benefit, even a little, to another section of the world's population, we will feel satisfied. But even if we fail to achieve that, we would still feel happy if in our travels to other parts of the world we encounter your hands of friendship, remembering this two-month stay in Cuba. [*Applause*]

Compañeros, we have fond memories of you. We look forward to meeting you again. We invite you to visit our country as often as you like, to work here, to learn here, or simply to see it again. We bid you farewell with a brotherly hug and say to you, "Until we meet again!" [*Ovation*]

The university must color itself black, mulatto, worker and peasant

At the Central University of Las Villas
December 28, 1959

When the revolution triumphed in January 1959, the class composition of the student body and faculty at Cuba's three universities—located in Havana, Santiago de Cuba, and Santa Clara—reflected the exploitative society Cuban workers and peasants were now striving to leave behind.

From its earliest days, Cuba's revolutionary government instituted measures to begin redressing these class inequalities and the racist discrimination inherent in capitalist social relations, exacerbated in Cuba by more than three centuries of black slavery and decades of U.S. imperialist domination. In addition to the agrarian reform and nationalization of industry, the new government carried out numerous other revolutionary measures during its first two years. It mobilized more than a hundred thousand young people as volunteer teachers who spread out across rural Cuba in a one-year campaign that virtually eliminated illiteracy—a scourge that prior to the revolution was a fact of life for nearly 25 percent of the people. Government decrees slashed rents and the cost of

Che Guevara at Central University in Las Villas December 28, 1959, receiving honorary degree and cap and gown from university rector Mariano Rodríguez.

"I can only accept the degree as a tribute to our army of the people, since the only education I have imparted has been that of guerrilla camps, swearwords, and fierce example. That is why I continue to wear my Rebel Army uniform."

medicines in half and reduced electricity and phone rates. An extensive and universal public education system was established for the first time in Cuba, while private schools were turned into centers of education for all. A public health system was inaugurated with free medical care for the entire population.

In the following speech presented at the Central University of Las Villas in Santa Clara, and in the subsequent two items in this book, Che Guevara addresses the challenge of advancing this course in Cuba's universities too, opening up these virtually all-white enclaves to sons and daughters of workers and peasants, and transforming their character and curriculum in line with the new revolutionary tasks.

A system of racial segregation stigmatizing blacks and mulattos was reproduced daily by the workings of capitalism in prerevolutionary Cuba. Africans had been brought to Cuba as early as the Spanish conquest in the 1500s, toiling as slaves on sugar plantations. The wars to win the island's independence from Spain in the latter nineteenth century were intertwined with the fight to abolish slavery, which was eliminated only in 1886. Tens of thousands of slaves and their descendants fought as soldiers, officers, and commanders in the three wars for independence, constituting the majority of the members of the Liberation Army.

Throughout the first six decades of the twentieth century, blacks in Cuba faced the worst conditions in city and countryside, whether in employment, education, health, or housing. A system of racial segregation similar to that in the Jim Crow South of the United States prevailed across much of Cuba. Among the first steps of the new revolutionary government were laws that confronted this racist oppression. Speaking to a rally in Havana on March 22, 1959, Fidel Castro announced that discrimination against blacks in employment had been outlawed. Several weeks later, Law 270 declared all beaches and other public facilities open to everyone—black, mulatto, or white. Clubs, businesses, and other establishments that refused equal access and service to blacks were closed. These laws were enforced by the Rebel Army, the newly formed revolutionary police force, and the popular militias.

As noted by Guevara in the speech that follows, his visit to Las Villas coincided with the First National Forum of Cuban Industries, organized by university students there. Since October 1959, Guevara had headed the Department of Industrialization of the National Institute of Agrarian Reform. On November 26, 1959, he was appointed president of the National Bank as well.

~

Dear compañeros; new colleagues in the Faculty Senate and old colleagues in the struggle to liberate Cuba:

I must begin my talk by stating that I can only accept the degree bestowed upon me today as a general tribute to our people's army. I cannot accept it as an individual for the simple reason that anything that is not what it claims to be lacks any value in the new Cuba. How could I as an individual, Ernesto Guevara, accept the degree of Doctor Honoris Causa conferred by the School of Education, since the only education I have imparted has been that of guerrilla camps, swearwords, and fierce example? [Applause] And I believe such things certainly cannot be transformed into a cap and gown. That is why I continue to wear my Rebel Army uniform, even as I come and sit before you in this Faculty Senate, in the name and on behalf of our army. In accepting this designation—which is an honor for us all—I also wanted to present our message, that of a people's army, a victorious army.

I once promised the students at this campus a brief talk

presenting my views on the role of the university. Work, however, and a mountain of events prevented me from doing so. But today I am going to do it, bolstered moreover by my status as Professor Honoris Causa. [*Applause*]

So what must I say about the university's fundamental duty, its article number one, in this new Cuba? What I must say is that the university should color itself black and color itself mulatto—not just as regards students but also professors. It should paint itself the color of workers and peasants. It should paint itself the color of the people, because the university is the patrimony of no one but the people of Cuba. If this people, whose representatives occupy all the government posts, rose up in arms and broke through the dikes of reaction, it was not because those dikes lacked flexibility. Nor did reaction lack the basic intelligence to be flexible in order to slow the people's advance. Nevertheless, the people triumphed. And they are somewhat spoiled by their victory. They are conscious of their own power, that they are unstoppable. Today the people stand at the door of the university, and it is the university that must be flexible. It must color itself black, mulatto, worker, peasant, or else find itself without doors. And then the people will smash their way in and paint the university with the colors they see fit.

That is the first message—one I would have liked to express in the first days following the victory, [*applause*] in all three universities of the country, but was only able to do so at the University [of Oriente] in Santiago. If you were to ask my advice on behalf of the people and the Rebel Army, and as a professor of education, I would say that in order to reach the people you must feel as if you are part of the people. You must know what the people want, what they need, and what they feel. You must do a little self-analysis, study the university's statistics, and ask how many workers, how many peasants, how many men who make their living by their sweat eight hours a day are here in this university.

Once you have asked yourselves this, you must also ask yourselves, by way of self-analysis, whether or not the government of Cuba today represents the will of the people. If the answer is yes, if this government really represents the will of the people, [*loud applause*] then one must also ask the following: This government—which represents the will of the people—where is it at this university and what is it doing? We would then see, unfortunately, that the government representing virtually the totality of the Cuban people has no voice in the Cuban universities with which to sound the alarm, to provide words of guidance, and to express, free of intermediaries, the will, the desires, and the feelings of the people.

The Central University of Las Villas recently took a step forward to improve the situation. When it held its forum on industrialization, it turned not only to the Cuban industrialists but also to the government. We were asked our opinion and the opinion of all the technicians in the state and semi–state agencies. Because in this first year since liberation—and I can say this without boasting—we are doing much more than other governments did, and much, much more than those who pompously speak of themselves as "free enterprise." Therefore, we have the right to state that the industrialization of Cuba, which is a direct result of the agrarian reform, will be attained by the revolutionary government, and under its guidance. [*Prolonged applause*] Private enterprise will naturally play an important role in this stage of the country's growth. But the government will establish the guidelines, and will do so based on its own achievements. [*Applause*] It will do so because it raised the banner of industrialization in response to what is perhaps the most deeply felt aspiration of the masses, not in response to violent pressure from the country's industrialists. Industrialization, and the effort it entails, is the child of the revolutionary government, which will guide and plan it for that reason.

The ruinous loans of the so-called Development Bank have disappeared from here forever. This bank, for example, would loan 16 million pesos to an industrialist who would put up 400,000 pesos (and these are exact figures). These 400,000 pesos did not come out of his pocket either; they came out of the 10 percent kickback he received from the salesmen he purchased the machinery from. Even though the government had put up 16 million pesos, this gentleman who put up 400,000 pesos was the sole owner of the company. And since the government held his debt he could pay at easy terms and at his convenience. Now the government has stepped in, refusing to recognize this state of affairs. It claims for itself any company set up with the people's money. If "free enterprise" means a few spongers enjoy all the money of the Cuban nation, then this government states quite clearly that it is opposed to "free enterprise," to the extent the latter is opposed to state planning.

Since we have now ventured into the thorny area of planning, let me say that only the revolutionary government, which plans the country's industrial development from one end to the other, has the right to establish the type and quantity of technical personnel needed in the future to meet the needs of this nation. The revolutionary government should at least get a hearing when it says it only needs a certain number of lawyers or doctors, but it needs five thousand engineers and fifteen thousand industrial technicians of all types [*prolonged applause*]—and that they must be trained, they must be found, because this is the guarantee of our future development.

Today we are working tirelessly to transform Cuba into

a different country. But the professor of education standing before you today does not deceive himself; he knows that he is as much a professor of education as he is president of the Central Bank, and if he must perform one or another task, it is because the needs of the people require that of him. None of this is accomplished without the people themselves suffering, because we are still learning in each case. We're learning on the job. Since we hold new responsibilities and are not infallible—we weren't born knowing what to do—we must ask the people to correct the errors.

This professor standing before you was once a doctor, and by dint of circumstance was obliged to take up arms, and after two years graduated as a guerrilla commander—and will later on have to graduate as a bank president or a director of industrialization of the country, or perhaps even a professor of education. [*Applause*] This same doctor, commander, president, and professor of education wishes that the diligent and studious youth of the country prepare themselves so each of them in the near future may occupy the positions assigned them, without hesitation, and without the need to learn on the job. But this professor here before you—a son of the people, forged by the people—also wants this very same people to have, as a right, the benefits of education. The walls of the educational system must come down. Education should not be a privilege, so the children of those who have money can study. Education should be the daily bread of the people of Cuba. [*Applause*]

Naturally, it never occurred to me to demand that the current professors and students of the University of Las Villas perform the miracle of enrolling the masses of workers and peasants at the university. We still need to travel a long road, to go through a process all of you have lived through, a process of many years of preparatory studies.

What I do hope to accomplish, however, basing myself on my modest background as a revolutionary and rebel commander, is for the students at the University of Las Villas to understand that education is no longer anybody's exclusive preserve, and that this campus where you carry out your studies is no longer anyone's sheltered enclave. It belongs to the people of Cuba as a whole, and it will either be given to the people, or the people will take it. [*Applause*]

I began the ups and downs of my career as a university student, a member of the middle class, a doctor who shared the same horizons, the same youthful aspirations you have. In the course of the struggle, however, I changed and became convinced of the imperative need for revolution, and of the great justice of the people's cause. That's why I would hope that you, who are the masters of the university today, would turn it over to the people. I am not saying this as a threat that tomorrow the people will take it from you. No, I am simply saying that if the masters of today's University of Las Villas, the students, turn it over to the people as represented by their revolutionary government, that would be another of the many beautiful examples being set in Cuba today.

And to the professors, my colleagues, I have something similar to say to you: You must color yourselves black, mulatto, worker and peasant. You must go to the people. You must live and breathe as one with the people, which is to say, you must feel the needs of Cuba as a whole. When we achieve this, no one will be the loser. All of us will have won, and Cuba will be able to continue its march toward the future on a stronger footing.

And it won't be necessary to include, as a member of your faculty, this doctor, commander, bank president, and now professor of education, who bids you all farewell. [*Ovation*]

Above: University of Havana, July 1960. Tank, center foreground, was captured by university students from Batista forces. Banner announces revolutionary dance on August 6, including coronation of the "queen of the militia." **Below**: Guevara speaking to students at the University of Havana, November 27, 1961.

"I do not believe that education is what shapes a country. In fact, our Rebel Army, uneducated as it was, demonstrated the opposite. But neither is it true that economic transformation alone will transform education."

The role of the university in Cuba's economic development

At the University of Havana
March 2, 1960

The development of both agriculture and industry in Cuba, as elsewhere in Latin America, Africa, and most of Asia, was stunted by centuries of colonial exploitation compounded by decades of imperialist plunder. U.S. capital imposed a largely single-crop economy on the island—sugar. Cuba was bound by agreement to supply Yankee monopolies with what amounted to more than one-third of the sugar for the U.S. market. At the same time, Cuba was shut off from other buyers of its crop and was heavily dependent on imports from the United States for industrial products and even food.

Organizing Cuba's workers, peasants, and youth to blaze a trail out of this subjugation was the topic of Guevara's nationally televised speech to students at the University of Havana in March 1960, printed here. At the time, the U.S. House of Representatives was discussing a bill sent to congress by U.S. president Eisenhower authorizing Washington to reduce Cuba's sugar quota. The bill was passed July 3 and three days later Eisenhower slashed the quota.

Anticipating Washington's moves, the revolutionary government was negotiating trade agreements with other countries. These included a five-year pact with the Soviet Union that had been signed in mid-February, providing for the purchase of one million tons of sugar annually and the extension of low-interest loans to Cuba.

Imperialism was also stepping up acts of counterrevolutionary sabotage and terror. Planes taking off from Florida targeted Cuba's sugarcane fields and refineries. Two days after Guevara's speech, the ship La Coubre—carrying arms bought from Belgium with donations from Cuban working people to defend their revolution—blew up in Havana harbor, killing eighty-one people. At a mass rally the following day honoring those who died in the explosion, Fidel Castro proclaimed the new battle cry of the revolution *"Patria o muerte!"* [Homeland or death!]

~

My dear compañeros:

Before getting into the subject of today's conversation, I'd like to warn you not to put too much weight on Mr. Naranjo's words—I think that's the name of the person who introduced me. I'd rather you consider me a modest revolutionary and a first-year student. [*Applause*] I'm a freshman in economics at Revolution University. [*Applause*]

I have come to speak with you bearing the somewhat ambiguous title of revolutionary, as well as the title that unites us all as brothers: that of student.

I intended this conversation to be a little more informal, with questions and answers, and even debate. But the special circumstance that it is being televised to the entire country requires me to present the subject I was going to speak about in a more organized fashion. It is a subject that has been of concern to me, as I believe it should be to many of you.

Roughly, we might call this speech "The Role of the University in Cuba's Economic Development," because we are beginning a new stage in the area of economics.

We have achieved all the political prerequisites to begin this economic reform, and we have taken the first step along these lines, changing the structure of land ownership in our country. That is to say, we have started with an agrarian reform, as every development process should start.

But to know what this process will be, we have to situate ourselves historically and economically. If we are beginning a process of development, that means we are not developed. We must be underdeveloped, semicolonial, or semi-industrialized—as the most optimistic would have it; use whatever name you wish. But we must study in detail the characteristics of that system, what it is that makes us underdeveloped, and what are the measures that will enable us to overcome that underdevelopment.

Naturally, the first characteristic of an underdeveloped country is its lack of industry, its dependence on goods manufactured abroad. Cuba fully complies with this first prerequisite of being an underdeveloped country.

Why has Cuba for years had the appearance of prosperity when in fact we are without qualification a semicolonial country? Simply because Cuba's exceptional climate and the accelerated development of a single industry, sugar, made it possible for us to compete in the world market with favorable productivity levels in that industry. U.S. capital, trampling over the laws they themselves came up with, promoted the development of the sugar industry.

There's an old law from the times of the U.S. government

in Cuba that prohibited any U.S. citizen from owning land on the island. That's what the law says. Nevertheless it was soon broken. [Manuel] Sanguily's proposition to ban land ownership by foreigners could not go anywhere, and little by little these foreigners began to take over the large sugar plantations and to create this powerful industry of 161 mills, six million tons of sugar a year, and productivity rates that made it competitive on a world scale. But they were very careful to ensure that Cuba would maintain another essential feature of semicolonial countries: that of producer of a single product. So Cuba depends solely and exclusively on a single product to obtain foreign exchange with which to purchase consumer goods on the foreign market.

By bestowing on us the apparent gift of a higher price for sugar, they forced on us a market economy, ruled solely by the law of supply and demand. And in exchange for low U.S. tariffs, goods manufactured in the United States received preferential tariffs here, thus making it impossible for our own local industry, or for any non-U.S. manufactured goods, to compete.

From the beginning of the new nation, such sharp economic dependency translated into an almost absolute political dependency, even after the Platt Amendment was abrogated.[1] That political situation ended January 1, 1959. The first frictions and difficulties with the "northern giant" began immediately. These frictions were logical if you consider that a country accustomed to special treatment suddenly saw that this little "colony" in the Caribbean irreverently sought to speak the only language a revolution can speak: the language of equal treatment.

At first, that huge Uncle Sam was depicted in the comics as being somewhat amused and surprised, looking at

---

1. See glossary notes, Platt Amendment.

a little bearded dwarf who was trying to kick him in the shins, since he couldn't reach any higher. [*Applause*] But the bearded dwarf has been growing and growing, until he now reaches continental proportions. He is now a living presence at the dinner table of the owners of wealth on the continent. [*Applause*] So whenever a people seeks to express their discontent and their unwillingness to go along with being pillaged, they raise the banner so dear to us: the portrait of Fidel Castro. [*Applause*]

Politically we have gone the farthest of all the countries of America in redeeming our territory. Whether the great powers of this continent like it or not, it cannot be debated that we are the leaders of the people. [*Applause*] To the powerful masters we represent all that is absurd, negative, irreverent, and disruptive in this America that they so despise and scorn. But on the other hand, to the great mass of the American people (I'm referring to Our America, which is everything south of the Río Bravo[2])—these peoples derisively called "mestizos"—we represent everything noble, [*applause*] sincere, and combative.

But we know perfectly well that our economic development has yet to catch up with our political development—in fact, it has been left far behind. It is for this reason that the attempts at economic aggression being cooked up in the U.S. House of Representatives could have an effect, because we are dependent on a single product

---

2. The term "Our America" was first used by Cuban national hero José Martí, explaining the struggle for Cuba's independence as part of the broader struggle against U.S. imperialist domination of Latin America as a whole. The Río Bravo, commonly called the Rio Grande in the United States, forms the current border between the U.S. state of Texas and Mexico. Martí conceived "Our America" as encompassing everything from this point southward to Patagonia, on the extreme southern tip of the continent.

and a single market. So when we fight with all our might to free ourselves from this dependency and we sign an agreement to sell a million tons of sugar and for a credit of one hundred million dollars, or pesos, with the Soviet Union, [applause] the colonial representatives leap up to sow confusion. They try to prove that by selling to another country we are enslaving ourselves. But as far as slavery is concerned, they've never stopped to analyze what the regular sale of three million tons at supposedly preferential prices to the "northern giant" has meant, or means for the people of Cuba.

At the present time we must wage an economic fight to diversify our markets and our production, and we must wage a political fight to explain to our people why the Cuban Revolution is looking for new markets. The history of the type of laws being concocted in the U.S. House of Representatives can help us demonstrate how correct we were historically to move in anticipation of the aggression they were preparing, and to try to rapidly take our sugar to other markets.

But I have not come here to speak only about sugar. I would have preferred not to speak of it at all, because what we are trying to do is turn sugar into simply one of many Cuban products made by Cuban hands, in Cuban factories, to trade in all markets around the world. [Applause] And it is on this question and at this very moment that the role of technology and culture in our country's development becomes relevant and assumes its real significance. We are referring now to the role of our educational institutions in the future development of our nation.

I do not believe education is what shapes a country. In fact, our Rebel Army demonstrated the opposite. Uneducated as it was, it broke through numerous obstacles and prejudices. But neither is it true that economic develop-

ment alone—by the sheer fact of an economic transformation—will transform education, bringing it up to the same
level. Education and economic development are constantly
interacting and being reshaped. Even when we were able
to change the entire economic landscape of the nation, the
fact is that we have retained the same university structure.
So on a practical level, this problem has started to knock
on our doors. It is now knocking on the doors, for instance,
of the National Institute of Agrarian Reform.

With a stroke of the pen, we liberated our oil, and it
became Cuban. [*Applause*] We took the fundamental step
of freeing our mining industry, making it Cuban.[3] [*Applause*] We began a process of developing six branches
of production that are extremely important and basic:
heavy chemicals; organic chemicals, starting with sugar
hydrocarbons; mining; fuels; metallurgy in general and
steel in particular; and the byproducts of our intensive
agricultural development. But we face the sad reality that
the country's universities—both in terms of course matter and number of students—are not adequate to meet the
new needs of the revolution.

Just the other day compañero [Angel] Quevedo asked
me in a letter what I thought about having an economics school at the University of Havana. To respond to this
question, all we have to do is conduct a survey of the economists currently working in the state planning bodies. The
answer jumps out at you right away, in a somewhat aggres-
sive fashion. When all our economic advisers are Chil-

3. On October 27, 1959, the revolutionary government passed a law regu-
lating the extraction of mineral and oil reserves, which asserted Cuba's
sovereignty over its subsoil. Under the law, the government was given
the power to demand that any mine or refinery deemed essential to the
national interest be kept in production; a refusal to do so would give the
government the right to take it over.

eans, Mexicans, Argentines, Venezuelans, Peruvians, or other compatriots from Latin America—whether they've been sent to work for the ECLA [United Nations Economic Commission for Latin America] or INRA [National Institute of Agrarian Reform]—when, in fact, even our minister of the economy [Regino Boti] has been educated in universities abroad, the question of whether we need a school of economics has an obvious answer: the need is enormous. And we need qualified professors who are able to understand the rhythm and direction of our economic development, which is to say, the rhythm and direction of our revolution.

That is one example. But what if we had engineers in the mining industry, in the oil or chemical industries, who knew the truth because they learned the basics of chemistry here? It is a fact that, while the government is trying to develop each of the six basic branches of our industry in order to give them a new tone and a superdynamic push, we lack the executive hand consisting of technicians—and note that I'm not even saying revolutionary technicians, which would be the ideal thing—simply technicians, with whatever skills and ways of thinking they may have; regardless of all the ideological fetters and obstacles from the past they may carry. We don't even have this type of technician, who could help smooth out the road of the revolution.

But even more, at a time when all students should have as many resources as possible to help them achieve their goals and get their degrees, we find that a simple transfer from Santa Clara to Havana disrupts a student's education, because in this tiny country, the three universities have not even agreed to establish, as a minimum, a common program of study.

The government is taking steps and is conscious of where

they will lead. The entire people support these steps by the government, and you are training to defend with your bodies and blood the revolution that is the pride of Latin America today. Why then can't the universities march together on the same road and at the same pace as the revolutionary government? [*Applause*]

I don't want to come and argue in front of the cameras. I simply want to sound the warning bell so that thought is given to this: there cannot be two sets of principles nor can students have two sets of criteria. Anyone ready to give their life to defend the revolution should also be willing to help carry out the revolution's plans, [*applause*] which is much easier. Because, say what you may, it's much easier to adapt to another opinion than to die for an ideal.

That's why the university at this time takes on such extraordinary importance. Even though it is made up of individuals who in their majority support the government, in a way it can become an element that holds the revolution back. Right now you are not afraid of that; right now everything is rosy. But the day will come, tomorrow or the next day, when the lack of technicians will prevent the establishment of an industry and we'll have to postpone it for two, three, five, or who-knows-how-many years.

At that precise moment we will see how important this delaying factor has been—having a university that has not brought its lecture halls and classrooms up to the level demanded by the revolution, by the people.

Is this inevitable? Is it inevitable that, within a certain period of time, universities are doomed to become a brake, that is, virtual centers of counterrevolution? I reject that with all the strength of my revolutionary conviction, because the only thing we lack—absolutely the only thing—is coordination. Nothing more than that little word, which has become the goal of all government institutions, and

should also be the object of attention of the student compañeros. Coordination between the students of the University of Havana and the universities of Las Villas and
Oriente. Coordination between the programs of study of
these three universities and those of the institutes and
secondary schools that will supply them with students.
Coordination between all these student bodies and the
revolutionary government. Coordination so that at a certain moment, for example, the students know that at some
point in the future the government's plans for development will require a hundred chemical engineers. They will
take the necessary measures to organize the training of
these hundred chemical engineers who are needed. Coordination to avoid an excess of my colleagues, doctors, who
would vegetate in bureaucratic jobs, instead of carrying
out the great social function of medicine, attending only
to the struggle for life. Coordination so that the number
of graduates in those old fields of study called the humani-
ties are reduced to the amount necessary for the cultural
development of the country, and so that the student body
turns to those new fields of study that technology is showing us day by day, and whose absence today will be deeply
felt tomorrow.

This is the whole secret to success or failure—let's not say
failure—relative failure, the failure to achieve the plans of
the revolutionary government in the fastest way possible.
[*Applause*]

Right now, together with technicians from international
organizations and from the Ministry of Education, we are
studying the basis on which to establish technological institutes, which will provide us with an average scientific
foundation. That will help our development a great deal.
But no country can really call itself developed until it can
make all its plans and manufacture the majority of the

products necessary for its subsistence within its own borders. Technology will allow us to build things, but how to go about building them, to see farther down the road, is the job of planners. This is what must be studied in quality universities, with a broad cultural base, so that those coming out of the new university we all dream of will be able to answer the call of Cuba ten or fifteen years down the road.

Today in many posts we see a number of doctors, of professionals, carrying out bureaucratic tasks. Economic development has raised its finger and said: no more professionals are needed in these fields of knowledge. But the universities have shut their eyes to the warnings of the economic process and they have continued churning out this professional layer from their classrooms and lecture halls. We have to step back and carefully study the characteristics of development and then proceed to produce the new professionals.

Someone once told me that a profession was the result of vocation; that it was something innate and could not be changed.

First of all, I think that position is wrong. Statistically speaking, I don't believe that an individual example has any importance. But I began studying engineering and ended up a doctor; I later became a commander, and now you see me as a lecturer. [*Applause*] There are basic vocations, that's true, but today the branches of science are so vastly differentiated, on one hand, and so intimately tied together, on the other, that it is difficult for anyone to say at the dawn of their intellectual development what their true vocation is. Someone may want to be a surgeon and that will happen, and they'll be happy doing that their whole life. But along with him there will be ninety-nine other surgeons who could just as well have been dermatologists, or psychiatrists, or hospital administrators, depending on what an extremely demanding society enables them to be. Vocation can only play a tiny part in the choice of new professions being created or in the reorientation of those we already know. It can't be anything else, because other factors stand in the way. These are, as I said, the huge needs of a society; in addition, there is the fact that nowadays hundreds and thousands, and maybe even hundreds of thousands, of Cubans have had the vocation to be doctors or engineers or architects, or any other profession, but have not been able to do so simply because they could not afford it. In other words, among individuals, vocation does not play the decisive role.

I want to emphasize this, because it's typical in this modern world to have, on the one hand, a kidney specialist—speaking of a profession I'm familiar with—who often has little to do with an eye doctor, or an orthopedist. At the same time these three professionals, just like a chemist or a physicist, in order to understand the characteristics of matter, will have to study a series of things common to all. Today you have them talking about physical chemistry, and not just physics or chemistry, as perhaps they are still referred to in high school today and as I learned them in school. In order to understand physics and chemistry well, one has to know mathematics. In this way all professions are united in a single body of minimum knowledge that a student must have. Why assume then that a compañero who is just starting his first year of university studies already knows that after those seven years—or six, or five, or whatever—after completing a difficult field of study in which they learn things as of yet unsuspected, he will be an orthopedist, or a lawyer, or a criminologist? [*Applause*]

We should always think in terms of the masses and not in terms of individuals, without believing that we are anything other than individuals and jealous defenders of our individuality. To analyze and figure out the needs of a country, each of us must be able to defend our point of view a thousand and one times, if necessary. Still, it's criminal to think in terms of individuals because an individual's needs are completely unimportant in face of the human conglomerate of that individual's fellow countrymen. [*Applause*]

Speaking sincerely, I would have liked to present to you, compañero students, a series of facts and figures that would demonstrate the divorce that exists at this moment between the university and the needs of the revolution. Unfortunately, our statistics are rather poor and we don't have statisticians here; they just started to get organized and I couldn't present the proof of numbers to you—you who have minds accustomed to real, practical problems. This will have to wait for another time—if you have the patience you've had tonight. As for today, I will feel satisfied if after these words, you discuss the problem of the university, not with me but among yourselves, and with your professors and your fellow students at the universities of Oriente and Las Villas and also with the government, which means discussing it with the people. [*Applause*]

Che Guevara addressing international meeting of architecture students in Havana, September 29, 1963.

"There is a weapon in this mural — a U.S.-made M-1 rifle. When it was in the hands of Batista's soldiers that weapon was hideous. But that same weapon became extraordinarily beautiful when it became part of the arsenal of the people's army."

Never forget, technology is a weapon

To closing of First International Meeting of Architecture Students

September 29, 1963

The First International Meeting of Architecture Students and Professors took place September 27–29, 1963, on the eve of the Seventh Congress of the International Union of Architects held in Havana.

The final plenary session of the meeting of students and professors, which Guevara addressed, approved a number of resolutions, including a denunciation of Washington's indictment on September 27 of four U.S. young people for "conspiring" to travel to Cuba. Three of the youth were among fifty-eight people who earlier that summer had visited the island challenging the ban on travel to Cuba imposed by the administration of U.S. president John F. Kennedy. After a four-year fight against this antidemocratic move, the U.S. Supreme Court declared the travel ban unconstitutional in 1967.

Another resolution called for "active participation" by university students in their respective countries "in the struggles headed by the popular masses for deep-going transformations" of society. True political independence, the document said, could only be wrested in a "struggle against imperialism—headed by Yankee imperialism—and against colonialism," and would necessitate "replacing the decrepit socioeconomic structure with one that meets the interests of the entire working people, as the Cuban Revolution has shown."

As the congress of the International Union of Architects was concluding, the second major agrarian reform law, which confiscated holdings in excess of 165 acres, was enacted by the revolutionary government. This measure affected ten thousand capitalist farmers who owned 20 percent of Cuba's agricultural land and constituted an important base for counterrevolutionary activity organized by Washington. Through this measure, property relations on the land were brought into harmony with the state ownership of industry in Cuba, cementing the worker-farmer alliance that has been the backbone of the revolutionary regime from its inception.

Compañero students and professors of architecture the world over:

It is my duty to give the summary, as we call it in Cuba, that is, to make the closing remarks and conclude this international meeting of students.

I must begin by making a very embarrassing confession: I am totally ignorant on all these questions. My ignorance reached the point of not realizing that this international meeting of students was apolitical. I thought it was a student conference, without knowing that it was part of the International Union of Architects.

Therefore, as political people, that is, as students who participate in the active life of your country, and after reading the final resolutions of this meeting—which by the way shows that the ignorance was mutual because the resolutions are also very political [*laughter and applause*]—I thought I'd say, first of all, that I agree with the resolutions of this conference. It seemed to me that its conclusions were logical, not just revolutionary but also scientific—that is, scientific and revolutionary at the same time. So I was going to give a short speech, a slightly political one if you will. But I really don't know if this is the appropriate place to speak about political matters. At any rate you are the ones to decide whether I should do so, because I don't know much about technology. [*Applause and expressions of agreement*]

Okay. I am not resorting here to cheap demagogy in order to get around your rules. I did not know your rules and simply came to make a summary in my capacity as a politician, a politician of a new type, a politician of the people, but a politician nonetheless, due to my functions. I was also impressed that the conclusions were approved, it seems, by a very broad majority. I am in agreement with the vast majority of the resolutions; they outline the role of the student and the technician in society.

I was somewhat amazed by the resolutions, I can honestly tell you, because the people visiting us have come from every country of the world. There are only a few countries, numerically speaking, where socialism has been built, but in terms of inhabitants their numbers are strong.

The countries fighting for their liberation—under different systems and at different stages in their struggle—are many, but they also have different governments, and above all their professional layers do not always have the same interests. The capitalist countries, naturally, have their own ideology. For all these reasons, we were surprised by the tone of the discussions.

I thought, perhaps a bit mechanically, that in general students from most capitalist, colonial, and semicolonial countries belong to those layers of society whose economic resources place them outside the ranks of the proletariat, and that therefore, their ideology would be very far from the revolutionary ideology we hold in Cuba.

But my mechanical approach led me to forget that in Cuba also there was a layer of students, the majority of whom—given their social origins—did not belong to the proletariat either, yet that layer of students has participated in all the revolutionary actions in Cuba in recent times. They have given our people some of the most beloved martyrs in the cause of liberation. Some of them have now graduated, while others continue their studies, integrating themselves into the Cuban Revolution and giving it their total support.

I had forgotten there is something more important than the social class to which an individual belongs: youth, freshness of ideals, and a body of knowledge that, at the moment one emerges from adolescence, can be put at the service of the purest of ideals.

Later on, the social mechanisms that exist in the various oppressive systems one lives under may change this way of thinking. But students in their big majority are revolutionary. Students may have more or less awareness of a scientific revolution, they may be more or less conscious of what they want for their people or for the world and how to achieve it. But students are, by nature, revolutionary because they belong to that layer of young people for whom life is opening up in front of them, and they are acquiring new knowledge every day.

This is the way it has been in our country. And even though some professionals and students have clearly left us, we have seen with great satisfaction—and sometimes also with surprise—that the vast majority of students and professionals remained in Cuba in spite of all the opportunities they were given to leave the country, in spite of all the temptations offered by imperialism.

The reason is understandable: even if we keep in mind that under an exploitative social system students cannot choose their own career or follow their real inner vocation, there is always a meeting point between someone's inner vocation and the career chosen; only rarely does this not occur. As a rule, the choice of most careers is also influenced by a series of economic factors, although the choice is made primarily because of individual preference.

In our country professionals and students have been given the opportunity that a professional should really aspire to: the opportunity to have all the tools of their trade in order to accomplish their work. For the first time professionals in Cuba have felt themselves true builders of society, participants in society, responsible for society. They cease to be simple wage earners—partly hidden behind various forms of exploitation—but nevertheless in their great majority wage earners, building for somebody else, interpreting the wishes and opinions of others, always creating wealth for someone else through their work.

Clearly, in this beginning stage limitations have been great. Our scientists cannot carry out the research they would like. Sometimes we lack dyes and all kinds of technical devices they need to carry out their research. Our architects cannot design with all the taste and beauty they are capable of—they lack the materials to do so. It is necessary to distribute to the maximum what we do have, so that more can be given to those who have nothing. At this stage it is essential to redistribute wealth so that everyone has a little.

But very concretely, in exercising the profession you represent, the creative spirit of man is put to a test. There is the problem of the materials available and of the service to be provided, but it is up to our professionals to find the right solutions. In doing so, they have to carry out a fight as though they were fighting against nature, against an environment that is beyond man's control, in order to fulfill in the best possible way not only the desire to give more to our people, but also the personal satisfaction of building a new society with one's own hands, talents, and knowledge.

Our revolution has been characterized by broad-mindedness. We have not had the great problems with professionals that other countries building socialism have had, with debates on art. We have been very broad-minded.

We do not agree with everything our professionals and artists believe. Often we have had heated discussions with them, but we have taken those who are not socialists, those who not only don't care for socialism, but resent socialism and dream about the old days, and we have managed to have them remain in Cuba, fighting, discussing, working, and building. And, in fact, from a practical standpoint they are socialists, which is what we are interested in. [*Laughter*]

We have never fled from confrontation or discussion. We have always been open to discussing any idea. The only thing we don't allow is using ideas for purposes of blackmail, or sabotage against the revolution. In this respect we have been absolutely inflexible, as inflexible as anyone.

On the most basic level, our country has what is scientifically called the dictatorship of the proletariat, and we do not allow anyone to touch or threaten the state power of the proletarian dictatorship. But within the dictatorship of the proletariat there can be a vast field for discussion and expression of ideas. The only thing we demand is that the state's general policies in this stage of building socialism be respected. Such has been our approach.

Some professionals have gone to prison for direct counterrevolutionary acts, for sabotage. But even from prison they have been rehabilitated: they first work in jail; then, after their release, they work, and continue to work, in our industries. We trust them as completely as we trust any of our technicians. And they are reincorporated, even though they have known the harshest and darkest side of the revolution, which is repression. In a triumphant revolution repression is necessary because the class struggle does not end with the revolution's triumph. In our case, after the victory of the revolution the class struggle was sharpened to the maximum.

Acts of sabotage, assassination attempts—you probably noticed yesterday that they greeted us with a bomb right in the middle of the event.[1] They carried out their show of force—their counterrevolutionary fun. That's the way it's always been.

We attack and are relentless toward those who take up arms against us; it does not matter if these are outright weapons of destruction or ideological weapons to destroy our society. The rest, those who are dissatisfied, those who are unhappy yet honest, those who state that they are not socialist nor will they ever be, to them we simply say: "Before, no one ever asked you whether or not you were a capitalist—you had a contract and you fulfilled it. We say: fulfill your contract, do your work, espouse whatever ideas you like; we won't interfere with your ideas."

That is how we keep on building, with many problems, with many leaps backward. The revolution's road is not one of continuous successes, sustained advances, or rhyth-

---

1. A day earlier, an explosion was heard during Fidel Castro's speech to a mass rally in Havana on the third anniversary of the Committees for the Defense of the Revolution.

mic strides forward. At times we reach an impasse, when we lose revolutionary momentum, when we get disoriented. We have to regroup our forces, analyze our problems, analyze our weak points, and then march forward. That is how revolutions are made and consolidated. They are made the same way we began ours—by a group of men, supported by the people, in an area favorable for the struggle.

We have now reached the point where I must play the role of theoretician of something I know nothing about. With my limited knowledge, I will try to define what I understand an architect to be.

I believe an architect—as with practically every other professional—is a man in whom the general culture achieved by humanity up to that moment converges with humanity's general level of technology or with the particular technology of a given nation.

The architect, like every professional, is a man living within society. He can attend international apolitical meetings—and it's correct for them to be apolitical—to maintain peaceful coexistence. But I don't understand how, as a man, he can say he is apolitical.

To be apolitical is to turn one's back on every movement in the world. It is to turn one's back on who will be president or leader of a nation. It is to turn one's back on the construction of society, or on the struggle to prevent the new society from arising. In either of the two cases, one has to take a political position. In present-day society every one of us is by nature political.

The architect–political person—the convergence of the culture of humanity up to that point and its technology—confronts this reality.

Culture is something that belongs to the world. It belongs, perhaps as does language, to the human species. But

Che Guevara addressing the First Latin American Youth Congress in Havana, July 28, 1960.

"If this revolution is Marxist, it is because it discovered, by its own methods, the road pointed out by Marx."

JOSEPH HANSEN / MILITANT

COUNCIL OF STATE OFFICE OF HISTORICAL AFFAIRS

The first Agrarian Reform Law expropriated holdings over 1,000 acres, including giant plantations owned by United Fruit and other U.S. corporations. 100,000 peasant families received titles to the land they worked. **Above:** Peasant militia members march in Havana, April 1960. **Below:** Fidel Castro preparing to sign agrarian reform into law, May 17, 1959.

"How much capital do you need to begin an agrarian reform? None. The only capital needed is an armed people conscious of their rights."

"The forms of capitalism we have known, under which we have been raised and have suffered, are being defeated."

In July 1960 Washington announced decision to slash previously contracted sugar imports from Cuba. In August the revolutionary government responded to this assault by expropriating the property of U.S.-owned corporations in Cuba. **Above:** Cuban workers take over Texaco refinery, removing U.S. flag. **Below:** Participants in Latin American Youth Congress join Week of National Jubilation in Havana to celebrate nationalizations. Workers bearing coffins containing symbolic remains of U.S. companies march to waterfront and dump them into the sea.

The Cuban Revolution was part of a rising wave of anti-imperialist struggles. It inspired a new generation of toilers and youth worldwide, including those battling racist segregation in the United States. **Above:** Fighters for Black rights defy police attacks in Birmingham, Alabama, 1963. **Left:** Students in Paris occupying high school greet workers' demonstration during weeks of antigovernment actions in May–June 1968. **Facing page, top to bottom:** Anti–Vietnam War demonstration, New York City, 1967; Panamanians demand sovereignty over Canal, November 1959; demonstration in Algiers against French colonial domination, 1960. After eight years of revolutionary struggle the Algerian people won independence in 1962.

BOB ADELMAN

"We are
a mirror in
which the
oppressed
peoples of
the world
who are
fighting for
their freedom
see themselves
reflected."

"A Young Communist cannot
be limited by national borders.
You must practice proletarian
internationalism and feel it
as your own."

ORLANDO BORREGO / GRANMA

GRANMA

Since revolution's earliest years, Cuban internationalist volunteers have aided struggles of working people around the world. **Facing page, above:** Che Guevara (third from right) and other Cuban volunteers in training before departure for Bolivia, 1966. **Facing page, below:** Cuban teacher near Puerto Cabezas, Nicaragua, 1985. Following the victory of the Sandinista revolution in 1979, Cuba sent 2,000 teachers to Nicaragua. After two Cuban teachers were murdered by counterrevolutionaries in 1981, 100,000 in Cuba volunteered to take their place. **This page, above:** Cuban women's antiaircraft artillery unit, Angola, 1988. Aid was decisive in defeat of U.S.-backed aggression by South African apartheid regime in 1975–88 war. **This page, below:** Cuban volunteer doctor on horseback crossing river in Guatemala in wake of Hurricane Mitch, which resulted in thousands of deaths in Central America in 1998.

"Young Communists must be the first in work, the first in study, the first in defense of the country."

RAÚL CORRALES

Facing page: On eve of April 1961 Bay of Pigs invasion, Cuban antiaircraft unit trains to identify U.S. planes. **This page, above:** Havana "rally of the pencils" celebrates successful conclusion of year-long literacy campaign, December 22, 1961. Some 100,000 young people fanned out across Cuba to teach nearly a million peasants and workers to read and write, virtually eliminating illiteracy. **This page, below:** Members of Union of Young Communists join volunteer work brigade in Havana to repair housing, 1992.

This page, above: Cuban youth rally August 6, 1994, on Havana's seafront boulevard in support of the revolution, responding to antisocial actions and hijackings of boats for emigration outside legal means, encouraged by Washington. **This page, below:** Students in Stockholm, Sweden, protest attacks on education, February 1995. Sign reads, "We want to be able to continue our studies through higher education. We are the future." **Facing page, above:** March and rally for Puerto Rican independence, Guánica, Puerto Rico, July 25, 1998. **Facing page, below:** Striking U.S. workers picket poultry plant in Corydon, Indiana, 1999.

"Don't confuse the happiness,
the freshness, the spontaneity of youth
everywhere with superficiality."

BRIAN TAYLOR / MILITANT

KATHY MICKELLS / MILITANT

Above: Participants in 1996 U.S.-Cuba Youth Exchange meeting in Guantánamo, Cuba, discuss common struggles. **Below:** Kenia Serrano (right), then international relations secretary of the Federation of University Students in Cuba, talks with striking autoworkers at Caterpillar plant in York, Pennsylvania, during 1995 tour of United States.

> "Our youth must always
> be free, discussing
> and exchanging ideas,
> concerned with what
> is happening throughout
> the entire world."

technology is a weapon and should be used as a weapon, as everyone does.

We can show you this mural over here, for instance. There is a weapon in it, a U.S.-made M-1, a Garand rifle. When it was in the hands of Batista's soldiers and they were firing on us, that weapon was hideous. But that same weapon became extraordinarily beautiful when we captured it, when we wrested it from a soldier's hands, when it became part of the arsenal of the people's army. In our hands that weapon became an object of dignity. And without changing at all either its structure or its function of killing men, it acquired a new quality: now it was being used for the liberation of peoples.

Technology is the same. Technology can be used to subjugate peoples or it can be used to help liberate them. [*Applause*] That is one conclusion that flows from the document you approved.

In order to use the weapon of technology for society's benefit, one has to control society. To control society, the elements of oppression must be destroyed, and the social conditions prevailing in some countries must be changed. The weapon of technology must be placed at the disposal of all technicians, at the disposal of the people. That task belongs to all of us who believe that change is required in certain regions of the globe.

We cannot have technicians who think like revolutionaries but do not act like revolutionaries. There is an urgent need to make a revolution in most of our continents, in almost all of Latin America, in all of Africa and Asia, wherever exploitation has reached inconceivable degrees.

Whoever pretends that a technician, an architect, a doctor, an engineer, or any type of scientist should merely work with the instruments in his own specific field while his people starve to death or fall in battle, has in fact taken the side of the enemy. He is not apolitical, he is political—but in opposition to movements for liberation.

Naturally, I respect the opinions of all who are present here. Clearly there must be a few youth and many professionals here who think a socialist system, or what is known of it up to now, is a system of oppression, misery, and mediocrity—as is crudely stated and spread around in propaganda. They think that man can achieve full self-realization only when there is free enterprise, free thought, and all the things imperialism throws at us. Many of these people are honest in their thinking, and I am not here to argue. One cannot argue about these problems. For quite a long time, for generations, these people have been molded by the collective education capitalism has put in place in order to train its technical personnel. And had it not trained technical personnel faithful to its principles, it would already have fallen.

But it has begun to fall because the world is awakening. Today none of the old assertions are accepted any longer just because they were written long ago. Instead, people demand proof in practice of what is asserted; they want a scientific analysis of all assertions. Out of this dissatisfaction, revolutionary ideas are born and spread more and more throughout the world, backed by the living examples of how technology can be put at the service of man, as has happened in the socialist countries. That is what I could tell you on this.

I would like to add something directed to my compañeros, the students of Cuba. And since this will be about something a little bit specific, a little bit provincial for you, I beg you to simply not listen if it holds no interest for you. But we have to pay attention to our students, and we have to do this every single day.

Our young people were born in the midst of great turmoil. This is a country where not too long ago U.S. sailors performed their bodily functions on the head of our apostle [José] Martí's statue,[2] yet today our entire people stand firm against U.S. imperialism. An extraordinary phenomenon has occurred: a total change in the consciousness of the masses, with just a few years of revolutionary work. But as with any drastic and abrupt change, not everything is fully understood. So not everything is clear in the minds of our students. Their minds—unlike the minds of our people—are yet to free themselves from a whole number of apprehensions.

That is why we wanted to insist again at this moment of struggle—when we are facing Yankee imperialism directly, when it threatens us daily, when its aggressiveness is so clear—that the task of the students is more important than ever. They have to accelerate their studies in order to become the true builders of the new society. At the same time, they also have to deepen their consciousness so they know exactly how that society is to be built. So that they won't be mere builders without ideas, but rather, they will put their hands, their heads, and their hearts at the service of the society being born. And at the same time, they must be ready with rifle in hand, because the defense of our society is not a task that falls to only one or another layer in society. The defense of the Cuban Revolution is the continuous task of every Cuban at all times, in every trench.

Your task, compañero students, is to follow Lenin's ad-

---

2. On March 11, 1949, several members of the U.S. Navy were photographed climbing atop the statue of José Martí in Havana's Central Park, urinating on it. As word of the desecration spread, demonstrations quickly developed and there was a protest the following day led by the Federation of University Students (FEU) in front of the U.S. Embassy. Among the participants was the twenty-one-year-old law student Fidel Castro.

vice to the fullest: "Every revolutionary must be the best at his place of work, at his place of struggle." And your place of struggle today is the university; it is study, the training of our professionals as rapidly as possible in order to fill the gaps we have, to fill the holes left by imperialism when it took away our technical personnel, to confront the country's general backwardness, and to hasten the building of a new society.

That is the fundamental task, but not the only task. Because one should never put aside the conscious study of theory, or the possibility of having to grab a rifle at any moment, or the permanent necessity to defend the revolution with ideological weapons every minute of our lives.

This is a hard task, one in which we need to mobilize the strength of our students. This is a generation of sacrifice. This generation, our generation, will not have the goods, not even remotely, that the generations to come will have. We need to be clear on this, conscious of this, conscious of our role, because we have had the immense glory of being the vanguard of the revolution in the Americas. And today we have the glory of being the country imperialism hates the most. At every step we are in the vanguard of the struggle.

We have not renounced a single one of our principles. We have not sacrificed a single one of our ideals. Nor have we left unfulfilled a single one of our obligations. That is why we are in the vanguard, that explains the glory felt by every Cuban in each corner of the world he visits. But all this demands effort.

This generation—the one that has made the apparent miracle of establishing a socialist revolution a few steps from U.S. imperialism—has to pay for this glory with sacrifice. It must make sacrifices every day in order to build through its efforts the future you aspire to, the one you dream about, a future in which every resource, every means, every piece of technology, will be at your disposal so you can transform them and breathe new life into them and—if you will permit me to use this rather idealistic phrase—put them at the service of the people.

To do that, material goods must be produced, imperialism's attacks must be repulsed, and all difficulties must be confronted. That is why our generation will have a place in the history of Cuba, and a place in the history of Latin America. We cannot let down the hopes that all revolutionaries, all oppressed peoples in Latin America and perhaps in the world, have placed in the Cuban Revolution.

Furthermore, we must never forget that the power of the Cuban Revolution's example does not operate solely here at home. We have obligations that go far beyond the borders of Cuba. We have the obligation to bring the ideological flame of revolution to every corner of the Americas and to every corner of the world where we can get a hearing. We have the obligation to feel all the miseries occurring in the world, all exploitation and injustice. We have the obligation that Martí summed up in a phrase we have often used, and which we should post on the headboard of our beds, in the most visible place: "Every true man must feel on his own cheek the blow to the cheek of another."

That must sum up the ideas of the revolution in relation to every country of the world.

Our youth must always be free, discussing and exchanging ideas, concerned with what is happening throughout the entire world, open to using technology coming from any part of the world; welcoming whatever the world might offer us. And you must always be sensitive to the struggle, the sufferings, and the hopes of oppressed peoples everywhere.

This is how we will build our future.

Today, coming to the real and practical issues, let me say that you have quite a task in front of you. You are starting to hold congresses where technology will be the prime concern, and politics will disappear from the relations and the exchanges of experiences between men. But you, students of the world, should never forget that behind technology there is always someone controlling it; and that someone is society. You can either be for or against that society. There are those in the world who think that exploitation is good and there are those who think it is bad and must be ended. And even when there is no discussion of politics, a political being cannot renounce this inherent aspect of the human condition.

Never forget that technology is a weapon. If you feel the world is not as perfect as it should be, then you must struggle to put the weapon of technology at the service of society. You must rescue society before that can be accomplished, so that technology benefits the greatest number of human beings possible, so that we can build the society of tomorrow—whatever name you choose to give it—the society we dream of and that we call—as it was called by the founder of scientific socialism—communism.

Patria o muerte! [Homeland or death]
Venceremos! [We will win]
[*Ovation*]

What a Young Communist should be

On the second anniversary of the unification
of the revolutionary youth organizations

October 20, 1962

In December 1959 the Rebel Army's Department of Instruction, headed by Che Guevara, launched a revolutionary youth organization, the Association of Rebel Youth (AJR). In October 1960 the AJR fused with other revolutionary-minded youth groups, thus bringing together within its ranks young people from three organizations: the July 26 Movement; the youth wing of the Popular Socialist Party; and the March 13 Revolutionary Directorate. In April 1962 the AJR adopted the name Union of Young Communists (UJC).

The second anniversary celebration took place on the eve of the October 1962 "missile" crisis instigated by Washington. In April 1961 Cuba's Revolutionary Armed Forces and popular militia had dealt Washington its first military defeat in the Americas at Playa Girón on the Bay of Pigs. The U.S. rulers, however, continued to believe they could overthrow the revolutionary government and prepared for new military action against Cuba, with the direct participation of the U.S. armed forces. Operation Mongoose, under the direct super-

Che Guevara (above) and Joel Iglesias, then UJC president, addressing meeting to celebrate second anniversary of the unification of the revolutionary youth organizations, October 20, 1962.

"Youth must build a future in which work will be man's greatest dignity, a social duty, a delight; the most creative activity there is."

vision of U.S. attorney general Robert Kennedy, was set up by the White House in November 1961 to conduct covert operations in preparation for an invasion. In face of the growing threat, the Cuban government reached a mutual defense agreement with the Soviet Union in August 1962. The pact included the installation of Soviet-controlled nuclear-armed missiles on the island.

On October 22 U.S. president Kennedy publicly demanded removal of the Soviet missiles. Washington ordered a naval blockade of Cuba, accelerated its invasion preparations, and placed U.S. armed forces on nuclear alert. The determination of Cuba's workers and farmers—who mobilized in the millions to defend their revolution—stayed the hand of the Kennedy administration. Some 260,000 soldiers in regular units and 140,000 in support tasks took up arms and occupied their places in the trenches. Together with them were 42,000 Soviet troops. The rest of the population took up their assigned posts in production and basic services. Top Pentagon officials, whose intelligence services underestimated the number of Cuban and Soviet troops by half, informed Kennedy to expect as many as 18,000 U.S. casualties during the first ten days alone of an attempted invasion. Fearing the domestic political consequences of such stunning casualties, Washington backed off its imminent invasion plans.

On October 28, following an exchange of communications between Washington and Moscow, Soviet premier Nikita Khrushchev, without consulting the Cuban government, announced his decision to withdraw the missiles. The revolutionary government responded with indignation to the agreement reached without its participation, and on behalf of the Cuban people put forward a series of measures that would be necessary for a just and lasting normalization of relations between Washington and Havana.

Also speaking at the second anniversary meeting was Joel

Iglesias, the president of the UJC. Iglesias had joined the Rebel Army in May 1957 at the age of fifteen, earning the rank of commander. He had headed the commission that worked under Guevara's guidance to prepare the founding of the AJR.

~

Dear compañeros:

One of the most pleasant tasks of a revolutionary is observing how, over the years of revolution, the institutions born at the very beginning are taking shape, being refined, and strengthened; how they are being turned into real institutions with power, vigor, and authority among the masses. Those organizations that started off on a small scale with numerous difficulties and hesitations became, through daily work and contact with the masses, powerful representatives of today's revolutionary movement.

The Union of Young Communists, under different names and organizational forms, is almost as old as the revolution itself. At the beginning it emerged out of the Rebel Army—perhaps that's also where it got its initial name. But forging an organization linked to the army, in order to introduce Cuba's youth to the massive task of national defense, was the most urgent problem at the time and the one requiring the most rapid solution.

The Association of Rebel Youth and the Revolutionary National Militia grew out of what was formerly the Rebel Army's Department of Instruction. Later, each took on a life of its own. One became a powerful formation of the armed people, representing the armed people, with its own character but united with our army in the tasks of defense. The other became an organization whose purpose was the political development of Cuban youth.

Later, as the revolution was consolidated and we were able to lay out the new tasks before us, Compañero Fidel proposed changing the name of the organization, a name change that is an expression of principle. The Union of Young Communists [*applause*] has its face to the future. It is organized with the bright future of socialist society in mind, after we travel the difficult road we are now on of constructing a new society, then the road of completely solidifying the class dictatorship expressed through socialist society, until we finally arrive at a society without classes, the perfect society, the society you will be in charge of building, guiding, and leading in the future. And toward that end, the Union of Young Communists raises as its symbols those of all Cubans: study, work, and the rifle. [*Applause*] And on its emblem appear two of the finest examples of Cuban youth, both of whom met tragic deaths before being able to witness the final results of this battle we are all engaged in: Julio Antonio Mella and Camilo Cienfuegos. [*Applause*]

On this second anniversary, at this time of feverish construction, of ongoing preparations for the country's defense, and of the speediest possible technical and technological training, we must always ask ourselves first and foremost: What is the Union of Young Communists and what should it be?

The Union of Young Communists should be defined by a single word: vanguard. You, compañeros, must be the vanguard of all movements, the first to be ready to make the sacrifices demanded by the revolution, whatever the nature of those sacrifices may be. You must be the first in work, the first in study, the first in defense of the country. You must view this task not just as the full expression of Cuba's youth, not just as a task of the organized masses, but as the daily task of each and every member of the

Union of Young Communists. And to do that, you have to set yourself real, concrete tasks, tasks in your daily work that won't allow the slightest letup.

The job of organizing must constantly be linked to all the work carried out by the Union of Young Communists. Organization is the key to grasping the initiatives presented by the revolution's leaders, the many initiatives proposed by our prime minister, and the initiatives coming from the working class, which should also lead to precise directives and ideas for subsequent action. Without organization, ideas, after some initial momentum, start losing their effect. They become routine, degenerate into conformity, and end up simply a memory. I raise this warning because too often, in this short but rich period of our revolution, many great initiatives have failed. They have been forgotten because of the lack of an organizational apparatus needed to keep them going and bring them to fruition.

At the same time, each and every one of you should know that being a Young Communist, belonging to the Union of Young Communists, is not a favor someone has done for you. Nor is it a favor you are doing for the state or for the revolution. Membership in the Union of Young Communists should be the highest honor for a young person in the new society, an honor you fight for every minute of your lives. In addition, the honor of remaining a member of the Union of Young Communists and maintaining a high standing in it should be an ongoing effort. That is how we will advance even faster, as we become used to thinking collectively and acting on the initiatives of the working masses and of our central leaders. At the same time, in everything we do as individuals, we should always be making sure our actions will not tarnish our own name or the name of the association to which we belong.

Now, two years later, we can look back and observe the results of our work. The Union of Young Communists has tremendous achievements—defense being one of the most important and spectacular.

Those young people, or some of them, who first climbed the five peaks of Turquino,[1] others who were enrolled in a whole series of military organizations, all those who picked up their rifles at moments of danger—they were ready to defend the revolution each and every place where an invasion or enemy action was expected. The young people at Playa Girón were worthy of the high honor of being able to defend our revolution.[2] [*Applause*] At Playa Girón they had the honor of defending the institutions we have created through sacrifice, defending what the people have accomplished over years of struggle. Our entire revolution was defended there in seventy-two hours of battle. The enemy's intention was to create a sufficiently strong beachhead there, with an airfield that would allow it to attack our entire territory. They intended to bomb mercilessly, reduce our factories to ashes and our means of communication to dust, ruin our agriculture—in a word, to sow chaos across the country. But our people's decisive action wiped out that imperialist attack in just seventy-two hours. There, young people, many of them still children, covered themselves with glory. Some of them are here as examples of that heroic youth. As for others, only their memory remains, spurring us on to new battles that we will surely have to fight, to new heroic responses in the face of imperialist attack. [*Applause*]

At the moment when the country's defense was our

---

1. See glossary notes, Turquino.

2. See glossary notes, Bay of Pigs.

most important task, the youth were there. Today, defense is still at the top of our concerns. But we should not forget that the watchword that guides the Young Communists [study, work, and rifle] is a unified whole. The country cannot be defended with arms alone, with just our preparedness. We must also defend the country by building it with our work and preparing the new technical cadres to speed up its development in the coming years. These tasks are now enormously important, and are on the same level as the use of weapons themselves. When these problems were raised, the youth once again were there. Youth brigades, responding to the call of the revolution, invaded every corner of the country. And so, after a few months of hard battle in which there were additional martyrs of our revolution—martyrs in education—we were able to announce something new in Latin America: Cuba was a territory of the Americas free of illiteracy.[3] [*Applause*]

Study at all levels is also a task of today's youth; study combined with work, as in the case of those students picking coffee in Oriente, [*applause*] using their vacations to pick that bean so important to our country, to our foreign trade, and to ourselves, who consume a tremendous amount of coffee every day. That task is similar to the literacy campaign. It is a task of sacrifice that is carried out joyfully, bringing student compañeros together once more in the mountains of our country, taking their revolutionary message.

But this task is very important, because in this work the UJC, the Young Communists, not only give but receive. In some cases they receive more than they give. They gain new experiences: new experiences in human contact, new

---

3. See glossary notes, Literacy Campaign.

experiences in seeing how our peasants live, in learning what work and life are like in the most remote places, in everything that has to be done to bring those areas up to the same level as the cities and to make the countryside a better place to live. They receive experience and revolutionary maturity. And compañeros who carry out the tasks of teaching reading and writing or picking coffee, of being in direct contact with our people, helping them while far away from home, receive much more than they give—I myself can vouch for this. And they give a lot!

This is the kind of education that best suits youth who are being educated for communism. It is a kind of education in which work ceases to be an obsession, as it is in the capitalist world, and becomes a pleasant social duty, done joyfully to the rhythm of revolutionary songs, amid the most fraternal camaraderie and human relationships that raise us all up and give us new energy.

In addition, the Union of Young Communists has advanced a lot on the organizational level. There is a big difference between that weak embryo that was formed as a branch of the Rebel Army and this organization today. There are Young Communists all over, in every workplace, in every administrative body. Wherever they can have an effect, there they are, Young Communists working for the revolution. The organizational progress must also be considered an important achievement of the Union of Young Communists.

Nevertheless, compañeros, there have been many problems along this hard road, great difficulties, gross errors, and we have not always been able to overcome them all. It is obvious that the Union of Young Communists, as a younger organization, a younger brother of the Integrated Revolutionary Organizations [ORI], must drink from the fountain of experience of compañeros who have worked longer in all the tasks of the revolution. And it is obvious they should always listen, and listen with respect, to the voice of that experience. But youth must also create. Youth who do not create are a true anomaly. And the Union of Young Communists has been a bit lacking in that creative spirit. Through its leadership it has been too docile, too respectful, and not decisive in addressing its own problems. That is now breaking down. Compañero Joel [Iglesias] was telling us about the initiatives regarding work on state farms. That is an example of how total dependency on the older organization, which is becoming absurd, is beginning to break down, of how the youth are beginning to think for themselves.

Because we, and our youth along with us, are recovering from a disease that fortunately did not last very long but had a lot to do with holding back the ideological development of our revolution. We are all convalescing from the disease called sectarianism.[4] And what did sectarianism lead to? It led to mechanical imitation; it led to formal analyses; it led to separation of the leadership from the masses. It led to these things even within our National Directorate, and this had a direct reflection here in the Union of Young Communists.

If, disoriented by sectarianism, we were unable to hear the voice of the people, which is the wisest and most in-

---

4. On March 26, 1962, Fidel Castro gave a televised speech that became known internationally by the title "Against Bureaucracy and Sectarianism." In it he attacked the bureaucratic practices that led to sectarianism in the organizing and functioning of the ORI, then in the process of formation, which if allowed to continue would lead to the alienation of masses of workers and peasants. In the speech, Castro announced that Aníbal Escalante, a former leader of the Popular Socialist Party and organization secretary of the ORI, was being removed from his post. A process of reorganizing the ORI began.

structive voice, if we were unable to feel the pulse of the people so we could turn that pulse into concrete ideas, precise guidelines, then even less could we transmit these guidelines to the Union of Young Communists. And since the dependency was absolute and the docility very great, the Union of Young Communists was like a small boat adrift, depending upon the big ship, our Integrated Revolutionary Organizations, which was also adrift. So, the Union of Young Communists took a series of minor initiatives, all it was capable of then, which at times became transformed into crude slogans, manifestations of a lack of political depth.

Compañero Fidel made serious criticisms of the kind of extremism and sloganeering well known to all of you, such as "The ORI is the greatest!" and "We are socialists, go, go, go! . . ." All those things that Fidel criticized and that you are so familiar with were a reflection of the illness affecting our revolution. That era is over. We have completely eliminated it.

Nevertheless, organizations always lag behind a bit. It's like a disease that has rendered a person unconscious. Once the illness breaks, the brain recuperates and mental clarity returns, but the arms and legs remain slightly uncoordinated. Those first days after getting out of bed, walking is unsteady, then little by little becomes surer. That is the road we are now on. And we must objectively assess and analyze all our organizations so we can continue our housecleaning. So as not to fall, not to trip and fall to the ground, we must realize that we are still walking unsteadily. We must understand our weaknesses in order to eliminate them and gain strength.

This lack of initiative is due to a long-standing ignorance of the dialectic that moves mass organizations, forgetting that an organization like the Union of Young

Communists cannot be just a leadership organization that sends directives to the ranks all the time and doesn't listen to anything they have to say. It was thought that the Union of Young Communists, that all Cuba's organizations, had one-way lines, one-way lines of communication from the leadership to the ranks, without any line that went the other way and brought communication back from the ranks. Yet it was through a constant two-way exchange of experiences, ideas, and directives that the most important guidelines—those that could focus the work of our youth—would have to emerge, at the same time identifying the places where our work was weakest, the areas where we were failing.

We still see today how the youth—heroes, almost like in the novels—who can give their lives a hundred times over for the revolution, who can respond massively to whatever specific task they are called upon to do, nevertheless sometimes do not show up at work because they had a Union of Young Communists meeting. Or because they stayed up late the night before discussing some initiative of the youth organization. Or sometimes for no reason at all, with no justifiable reason. So when someone looks around at a volunteer work brigade to see where the Young Communists are, it often turns out there are none; they haven't shown up. The leader had a meeting to attend, another was sick, still another was not fully informed about the work.

The result is that the fundamental attitude, the attitude of being a vanguard of the people, of being that moving, living example that drives everybody forward as the youth at Playa Girón did—that attitude is not duplicated at work. The seriousness that today's youth must have in meeting its great commitments—and the greatest commitment is the construction of socialist society—is not reflected in actual work. There are big weaknesses and we must work on them, work at organizing, work at identifying the spot that hurts, the area with weaknesses to be corrected. We must also work so that each one of you achieves a clear consciousness that you cannot be a good communist if you think about the revolution only at the moment of decisive sacrifice, at the moment of combat, of heroic adventure, at moments that are out of the ordinary, yet in your work you are mediocre or less than mediocre. How can that be?

You already bear the name Young Communists, a name we as a leadership organization, as a leadership party, do not yet have. You have to build a future in which work will be man's greatest dignity, a social duty, a delight, the most creative activity there is. Everyone will be interested in their work and the work of others, in society's daily advance. How can it be that you who today bear that name disdain work? There is a flaw here, a flaw in organization, in clarifying what work is.

This is a natural human flaw. People—all of us, it seems to me—much prefer something that breaks the monotony of life, something every once in a while that suddenly reminds us of our own personal worth, of our worth within society. I can imagine the pride of those compañeros who were manning a *cuatro bocas*,[5] for example, defending their homeland from Yankee planes. Suddenly, one of them is lucky enough to see his bullets hit an enemy plane. Clearly, that is the happiest moment of a man's life, something never to be forgotten. And those compañeros who lived through that experience will never forget it. But we have to defend our revolution, the revolution we are building, day in and

---

5. Literally "four mouths," this was the popular term in Cuba for the Chinese-made ZPU-4 14.5-mm. antiaircraft heavy machine gun. The weapon had four barrels mounted on a four-wheel carriage.

day out. And in order to defend it we have to make it, build it, strengthen it, through the work that youth today don't like—or at the very least they put at the end of their list of duties. That is an old-fashioned mentality that dates back to the capitalist world, where work was indeed a duty and a necessity, but a sad duty and sad necessity.

Why does that happen? Because we still have not been able to give work its true content. We have not been able to link the worker with the object of his labor; and at the same time, imbue the worker with a consciousness of the importance of that creative act that he performs every day. The worker and the machine, the worker and the object to which he applies his labor—these are still different and antagonistic things. And that has to be changed, because new generations must be formed whose main interest is work and who know how to find in work a permanent and constantly changing source of fresh excitement. They need to make work something creative, something new.

That is perhaps the weakest point in our Union of Young Communists today, and that is why I am insisting on it. That's why, amid the happiness of celebrating your anniversary, I am adding a small bitter drop in order to touch that sensitive spot, and to call on the youth to respond.

Earlier today we had a meeting at the Ministry [of Industry] to discuss emulation.[6] Many of you have probably

---

6. Emulation is a form of contest among cooperating groups of workers, a contest among collective entities, to see which factory or enterprise can produce the most, with the greatest productivity and of the highest quality. The opposite of competition among individual workers—the dog-eat-dog condition of life and work under capitalism—emulation is only possible when workers are producing for themselves, not for their exploiters. It was tirelessly promoted by Che Guevara in factories under the direction of the Ministry of Industry in the early 1960s. "Emulation is a fraternal competition. . . . It is a weapon to increase production," he

already discussed emulation at your workplaces and have read that long paper about it. But what is the problem with emulation, compañeros? The problem is that emulation cannot be led by papers that contain production rates and orders and that put forward a model. Rates and models are necessary later on in order to compare the work of enthusiastic people who are involved in emulation. When two compañeros begin an emulation, that is, each one seeking to produce more on his machine, after a while they find they have to set up some standards to measure who is getting the most out of his machine, to determine product quality, the number of hours worked, what condition the machines are in when they finish, how they maintain them, any number of things.

But if instead of giving these production standards to these two compañeros who are involved in emulation, all we do is give them to two others who are thinking only about getting home, then what good are they? What purpose do they serve? We often set production goals and develop models for something that does not exist. But models must have content. Production goals have to limit and define an already existing situation. They must be the result of emulation, carried out anarchically if you will, yes, but enthusiastically, overflowing in every workplace in Cuba. Then, automatically, the need for standards and goals will appear. But emulation to fulfill production goals, no. That's how we have dealt with a lot of problems. That's how formal we've been in dealing with a lot of things.

I asked at that meeting why the secretary of the Young Communists hadn't been there, or how many times he had been there. He had been there once or a few times,

---

stated in 1963. "But it is not only that. It is also a tool for deepening the consciousness of the masses. The two should always go together."

and other Young Communists had never attended. But in the course of the meeting, as we discussed this and other problems, the Young Communists and the local party unit and the [Federation of Cuban] Women and the Committees for the Defense of the Revolution and the union all naturally became very enthusiastic. Or at least they were filled with anger, with bitterness at themselves—with a desire to improve, with a desire to show they could do what has not been done: that is, motivate people. And suddenly everybody made a commitment that the whole ministry would become involved in emulation on all levels, that they would discuss production rates later, after they got emulation going, and that within two weeks they could present the concretes, with the whole ministry actively involved in emulation. That indeed is a mobilization. The people there have already understood and sensed—because each of those individuals is a great compañero—that there was a weakness in their work. Their dignity was wounded, and they went about taking care of the problem.

That is what has to be done, remembering that work is the most important thing. Pardon me if I repeat it once again, but the point is that without work there is nothing. All the riches in the world, all humanity's values, are nothing but accumulated work. Without that, nothing can exist. Without the extra work that creates more surpluses for new factories and social institutions, the country will not advance. No matter how strong our armies are, we will always have a slow rate of growth. We have to break out of this. We have to break with all the old errors, hold them up to the light of day, analyze them everywhere, and then correct them.

Now, compañeros, I wanted to share my opinion as a national leader of the ORI on what a Young Communist should be, to see if we all agree. I believe the first thing that must characterize a Young Communist is the honor he feels in being a Young Communist, an honor that moves him to let the world know he is a Young Communist, something he doesn't hide or reduce to formulas. He expresses that honor at all times, so it comes from the bottom of his soul, and he wants to show it because it is his greatest pride. In addition, he should have a great sense of duty, a sense of duty toward the society we are building, toward our fellow human beings, and toward all humanity around the world. That is something that must characterize the Young Communist. And along with that there must be deep sensitivity to all problems, sensitivity to injustice; a spirit that rebels against every wrong, whoever commits it; [*applause*] questioning anything not understood, discussing and asking for clarification on whatever is not clear; declaring war on formalism of all types; always being open to new experiences in order to take the many years of experience of humanity's advance along the road to socialism and apply them to our country's concrete conditions, to the realities that exist in Cuba. Each and every one of you must think about how to change reality, how to make it better.

The Young Communist must always strive to be the best at everything, struggle to be the best, feel upset when he is not and fight to improve, to be the best. Of course, we cannot all be the best. But we can be among the best, in the vanguard. We can be a living example, a model for those compañeros who do not belong to the Young Communists, an example for older men and women who have lost some of that youthful enthusiasm, who have lost a certain faith in life, and who always respond well to example. That is another task of Young Communists. Together with that there should be a great spirit of sacrifice, not only in heroic ventures but at all times, making sacrifices to help the next compañero in small tasks so he can finish his work, so he can do his work at school, in his studies, so he can improve in any way.

He must always pay attention to the mass of human beings he lives among. Every Young Communist must fundamentally be human, so human that he draws closer to humanity's best qualities. Through work, through study, and through ongoing solidarity with the people and all the peoples of the world, he distills the best of what man is. Developing to the utmost the sensitivity to feel anguish when a human being is murdered in any corner of the world and to feel enthusiasm when a new banner of freedom is raised in any corner of the world. [*Applause*]

The Young Communist cannot be limited by national borders. The Young Communist must practice proletarian internationalism and feel it as his own. He must remind himself and all of us—Young Communists and those aspiring to be communists here in Cuba—that we are a real and living example for all Our America. And not just for Our America, but also for the other countries of the world fighting on other continents for freedom, against colonialism, against neocolonialism, against imperialism, against all forms of oppression by unjust systems. He must always remember that we are a flaming torch. Just as we are all, individually, a mirror for the people of Cuba, we are also a mirror in which the oppressed peoples of Latin America and the oppressed peoples of the world who are fighting for their freedom see themselves reflected. We must be a worthy example. At every moment and every hour we must be worthy of being that example. That is what we think a Young Communist should be.

And if someone says we are just romantics, inveterate idealists, thinking the impossible, that the masses of people cannot be turned into almost perfect human beings, we will have to answer a thousand and one times: Yes, it can be done. We are right. The people as a whole can advance, wiping out all those little human vices as we have been doing in Cuba over these four years of revolution, improving themselves as we all improve ourselves daily, intransigently casting off all those who fall back, who cannot march to the rhythm of the Cuban Revolution. It must be so, it should be so, and it will be so, compañeros. [*Applause*]

It will be so because you are Young Communists, creators of the perfect society, human beings destined to live in a new world where everything decrepit, everything old, everything that represents the society whose foundations have just been destroyed will have definitively disappeared. To reach that goal we have to work every day, along the lines of improving ourselves; of gaining knowledge and understanding about the world around us; of inquiring, finding out, and knowing why things are the way they are; and always considering humanity's great problems as our own.

Thus, at any moment, on an ordinary day in the years ahead, after much sacrifice—yes, after seeing ourselves perhaps many times on the brink of destruction, perhaps after seeing our factories destroyed and having rebuilt them, after seeing the death, the massacre of many of us and rebuilding what is destroyed—after all this, on an ordinary day, almost without noticing it, we will have created, together with the other peoples of the world, our ideal: communist society. [*Applause*]

Compañeros, speaking to the youth is a very pleasant task. You feel able to communicate certain things, and you feel that the youth understand. There are many more things I would like to say to you about our common efforts, our desires, about how, nevertheless, many of them shatter in face of daily reality and how we have to start all over after moments of weakness, about how contact with the people—the purity and ideals of the people—fills us with new revolutionary fervor. There are many more things to talk about, but we too have duties to carry out.

By the way, I'll take this opportunity to explain to you why I'm saying good-bye to you, with an ulterior motive, perhaps. [*Laughter*] I'm saying good-bye because I am going to fulfill my duty as a volunteer worker at a textile factory. [*Applause*] We have been working there for some time now, involved in emulation with the compañeros of the Consolidated Spinning and Textile Enterprise in another textile plant, and we are also involved in emulation with the compañeros of the Central Planning Board, who work in another textile plant. I want to tell you honestly that the Ministry of Industry is in last place in the emulation. We have to make a bigger, greater effort, repeatedly, to move ahead, to meet the goal we ourselves set of being the best, of aspiring to be the best, because it hurts us to be last in socialist emulation.

What happened is simply what has happened to a lot of you. The emulation is cold, a little bit artificial, and we have not known how to get in direct contact with the mass of workers in that industry. We have a meeting tomorrow to discuss these problems and try to resolve all of them, to find a common ground, a common language, an identity between the workers from that industry and ourselves, workers from the ministry. After we do that, I am sure our output will increase, and we will be able to at least fight a clean, honorable battle for first place. At any rate, at next year's meeting we'll tell you what happens. So until then. [*Ovation*]

Youth must march in the vanguard

To closing of Ministry of Industry seminar on
'Youth and the Revolution'

May 9, 1964

In May 1964 members of the Union of Young Communists working in the Ministry of Industry organized a weeklong seminar on "Youth and the Revolution." They met in the ministry's auditorium six consecutive nights after work. The closing session was addressed by Guevara, who had headed the ministry since its creation in February 1961.

When the Ministry of Industry was formed, it was given authority over 287 enterprises with some 150,000 workers. Under Guevara's leadership, the ministry set about creating an integrated and centralized national structure of industrial enterprises, giving the working class greater leverage in determining economic and social priorities. Through this effort, the revolutionary government confronted many key challenges in leading the transition to socialism.

In organizing the planning and management of Cuban industry, Guevara emphasized that advances in the productivity of labor depended, first and foremost, on the transformation of the political consciousness of the working class as the toil-

PHOTOS: GRANMA

Guevara addressing seminar on Youth and the Revolution at the Ministry of Industry in Havana, May 9, 1964.

"The process of politicizing this ministry is under way." Without this,"it is a very cold and bureaucratic place, a nest of nit-picking bureaucrats and bores, from the minister on down, who are constantly tackling concrete tasks in order to search for new relationships and new attitudes."

ers carried out the revolutionary task of building socialism. As workers developed their technical and administrative skills and also organized volunteer work brigades to meet pressing social needs, they would develop new, communist attitudes toward work. "We can undertake the task of creating a new consciousness because we have new forms of relations of production," Guevara wrote in February 1964, a few months prior to the seminar. Cuba's legacy of imperialist-imposed economic backwardness did not bar this course, he insisted. "The development of consciousness can advance ahead of the state of the productive forces in any given country" once the means of production belong to society, no longer to individual owners.

The goal is that "man-as-commodity" cease to exist, Guevara explained in "Socialism and Man in Cuba" in early 1965. In the transition to socialism, man "starts to see himself reflected in his work and to understand his full stature as a human being through the object created, through the work accomplished. Work no longer entails surrendering a part of his being in the form of labor power sold, which no longer belongs to him, but represents an expression and extension of himself, a contribution to the common social existence in which he is reflected."

Guevara also helped to lead the ongoing political regroupment of revolutionary forces in Cuba. In 1961 the July 26 Movement had initiated a fusion with the Popular Socialist Party and Revolutionary Directorate, both of which had joined in the revolutionary overthrow of the Batista dictatorship. This process culminated in October 1965 in the founding of the Communist Party of Cuba, with Fidel Castro as first secretary of the party's Central Committee.

As in the previous speech, clarification of the political challenges Guevara addresses here, including the character and leadership of a revolutionary youth organization and its activities, was an indispensable part of advancing the fusion process.

⌇

Compañeros:

Some time ago, I was invited by the youth organization to give closing remarks to a series of presentations and discussions through which the organization was showing clear signs of life within the framework of the political work of the ministry.

I was interested in talking with you, giving you some of my opinions, because I have often had a critical attitude toward the youth—not as youth per se but as an organization. In general, however, my critical approach has not been backed by suggestions for practical solutions to the problem. In other words, my role has been something like a sniper, a role not in keeping with other responsibilities I have, including as a member of the leadership, of the party secretariat, and so forth. There have been conceptual questions over the character of a youth organization that we have never totally agreed on. We have always thought that the youth, as an organization, had somewhat of a mechanical approach. And in our opinion, this prevented it from becoming a genuine vanguard. Naturally, all these problems ended up being discussed for a long time.

The youth organization was in fact born under our direct guidance, in its first embryonic form, when the Association of Rebel Youth was formed, subordinate to the Rebel Army's Department of Instruction. Later on it separated off, acquiring its own political characteristics.

Although I held a critical attitude toward the youth, this attitude was not always accompanied by proposals for systematic and concrete work. This is a very complex problem because it relates to everything that involves the party's organization. From a theoretical point of view—and not just with regard to the youth—we have a series of concerns we still have not been able to fully resolve. What is the role of the party? I'm not talking about its role in abstract, general terms, with which we are all familiar. But what should the party's approach be in each of the various fronts where it has to function? To what degree does it participate in public administration? What should be its degree of responsibility? What should be the relationship, for example, between the various levels of public administration and the party?

These are problems that have not been set down in rules, and that we are all familiar with. They are problems that create frictions at various levels. Take the National Directorate [of the party] and the Council of Ministers—here the interdependence of the two bodies is clear, and often the individuals involved are the same. Beyond this, each of these bodies functions independently. Certain work habits are created in each, concepts that clash in real life, and for which we have yet to find practical solutions. Obviously, this also has to do with the fact that there are different conceptual approaches at work, none of which has been able to prove itself more efficient and rational than the other. In fact, these concepts come from analyzing the deep problems that have occurred inside the socialist camp—from the very moment the first socialist revolution triumphed, from the October Revolution of 1917 up to the present.

These concepts must be analyzed and studied in depth, particularly in light of the specific features of our revolution. This revolution began as a mass movement supporting an insurrectional struggle, without the formation of an organic party of the proletariat. It later merged with the party representing the proletariat, the Popular Socialist Party, which to that time had not been leading the struggle.

Owing to these characteristics, our movement is fully impregnated by the petty bourgeoisie, both on the individual level and politically. In the course of the struggle and the revolution, each of us kept evolving, since the majority of the revolution's leaders, in terms of their class background, come from the petty bourgeoisie, and some even from the bourgeoisie.

This kind of baggage gets dragged along for quite a period of time; it cannot just be cut out of the minds of men overnight. This was so even when the socialist character of the revolution was declared—it was a declaration after the fact; there already was a socialist revolution because we had wrested the majority of the key means of production. But politically we were not moving forward evenly in step with all the advances the revolution was making on the economic level and in certain ideological areas.

This characteristic of our revolution means we have to be very cautious in characterizing our party as the leader of the working class as a whole, and above all with regard to its concrete relations with each of the different administrative bodies, the army, the security apparatus, and so on.

Our party does not yet have statutes. Our party still is not even completely formed. So the question is: Why don't we have statutes? There is plenty of experience; that is to say, experience that goes back almost fifty years. So what is going on? The answer is that there are certain questions about this experience that we are still trying to come to grips with, questions to which you cannot just give a spontaneous or superficial answer, because they have extremely important implications for the revolution's future.

In Cuba the ideology of the old ruling classes maintains its presence through the consciousness of individuals, as I indicated earlier. In addition, it remains present because it is constantly being exported from the United States—the organizing center of world reaction—which physically exports saboteurs, bandits, propagandists of all sorts, and whose constant broadcasts reach the entire national territory with the exception of Havana.

In other words, the Cuban people come in permanent contact with imperialist ideology. This is then repackaged here in Cuba by propaganda outfits scientifically organized with the goal of projecting the dark side of our system, which necessarily has dark sides because we are in a transitional period and because those of us who have led the revolution up to now were not professional economists and politicians with a lot of experience, backed by an entire staff.

At the same time, they promote the most dazzling and fetishistic features of capitalism. This is all introduced into the country, and sometimes it finds an echo in the subconscious of many people. It awakens latent feelings that had barely been touched owing to the speed of the process, to the huge number of emotional salvos we have had to fire to defend our revolution—where the word "revolution" has merged with the word "homeland," has merged with defense of every single one of our interests. These are the most sacred of all things for every individual, regardless of class background.

In face of the threat of thermonuclear aggression, as in October [1962], the people came together automatically. Many who had never even done guard duty in the militias showed up to fight. Everyone was transformed in the face of this clear injustice. Everyone wanted to demonstrate their determination to fight for their homeland. This was also a decision by people faced with a danger from which they could not possibly escape by remaining neutral, since neither embassies nor anything else will be considered neutral by an atomic bomb; everything is annihilated.

That is how we have been advancing, by leaps, uneven leaps, the way all revolutions advance, deepening our ideology in certain areas, learning even more, developing schools of Marxism.

At the same time, we constantly worry about coming to positions that could stop the revolution's progress and introduce through the back door petty-bourgeois concepts or imperialist ideology by way of these critical attitudes about the party's tasks throughout the state apparatus. That is why the party is not yet properly organized today. That is why we have not yet achieved the necessary degree of institutionalization at the top levels of the state.

But we are also trying to address several other questions. We need to create something new, which we feel should precisely reflect the relationships that should exist between the masses and those in positions of power, both directly and through the party. We have made various trial runs along these lines: pilot projects of various types of local administration—one in El Cano, a different one in Güines, yet another in Matanzas. Through these trial runs we are constantly observing the advantages and disadvantages of all these different systems—which contain within them the germ of a higher type of organization—for the development of the revolution and above all for the development of centralized planning.

The work of the youth was conducted within the context of this vast sea of ideological struggles among distinct supporters of different ideas, even if there were no defined tendencies or currents. The youth organization began functioning first as an outgrowth of the Rebel

Army; later it acquired greater ideological depth, and then it transformed itself into the Union of Young Communists, which we could call the antechamber to party membership, which necessarily implies the obligation of acquiring a higher level of political education.

Faced with these problems, there was no real discussion, although some discussions were held on the role of the youth organization, from a practical standpoint. Should the youth organization meet for three, four, or five hours to discuss profound philosophical questions? They can do so—no one is saying this is forbidden. But it is simply a question of balance and of one's attitude to the revolution, to the party, and above all to the people. The fact that the youth are taking up questions of theory shows they have already achieved a certain theoretical depth. But if all they are doing is grappling with theoretical questions, it means the youth have not been able to get beyond a mechanical approach, and are confused about their goals.

There has also been talk about how youth are by definition spontaneous, joyful. So the youth—and I'm talking in general, not about the particular group in the ministry here—have organized joyfulness. Then young leaders set about thinking, what is it youth should be doing, since, by definition, it's supposed to be merry and fun. Precisely this was turning youth into old people. Why should a young person have to sit down and think about what youth should be?

They should simply do what comes to mind, and that, in fact, will be what youth do. But this wasn't what happened, since there was a whole group of youth leaders who had truly grown old. That's when this joy, this youthful spontaneity is turned into superficiality. So we have to be careful.

We should not confuse the happiness, the freshness, the spontaneity of youth all over the world—and especially

Cuban youth, because of the nature of the Cuban people—with superficiality. These are two absolutely different
things. It's possible and necessary to be spontaneous and
gay, but one has to be serious at the same time. So this is
one of the most difficult problems to resolve when presented for theoretical discussion. Because, simply put, this
is what it means to be a Young Communist. You shouldn't
think about how to be one, it has to come from within.

I don't know if I'm getting into deep, semiphilosophical
waters, but this is one of the problems we have discussed
the most. The main way the youth must show the way forward is precisely through being the vanguard in each of
the areas of work they participate in.

This is why we have often had certain little problems
with the youth: that they weren't cutting all the sugarcane
they should, that they weren't doing as much voluntary
labor as they should. In short, it is impossible to lead with
theories alone; and much less can there be an army composed only of generals. An army can have one general,
maybe several generals and one commander in chief if it
is very large. But if there's no one to go into the battlefield,
there's no army. And if the army in the field isn't being led
by those who have gone into the field themselves, who've
gone to the front, then such an army is no good. One of
the attributes of our Rebel Army was that the men promoted to lieutenant, captain, or commander—the only
three ranks we had in the Rebel Army—were those whose
personal qualities had distinguished them on the field of
battle.

The first two ranks—the lieutenants and captains—were
the ones who directed combat operations. So that is what
we need—lieutenants and captains, or whatever you want
to call them. You can take away the military titles if you
want—but the person leading must do so by setting the

example. To follow or to make oneself be followed can be a difficult task at times. But it's much, much easier than forcing others to do the walking, making them proceed along a trail still unexplored, a trail on which no one has taken a single step.

So the youth still need to take up the big tasks the government set forward, take them up as tasks before the masses, turn them into their own aspirations, and march along this road as the vanguard. Led and guided by the party, the youth must march in the vanguard.

The first qualitative change in our party occurred when all the bad leadership methods were abandoned, and exemplary workers, vanguard workers—those workers on the production front who could really speak with authority and who were also the ones going to the front lines— were elected to membership.[1] Although this was not the only change, and had to be followed up by a whole series of organizational measures, it marks the most important aspect of our transformation. There have also been a series of changes in the youth.

I want to emphasize one point—something I have emphasized continuously: stay young, don't transform yourselves into old theoreticians, or theorizers, maintain the freshness and enthusiasm of youth. You must learn to grab hold of the great watchwords of the government, internalize them, and become the motor force of the whole mass movement, marching in the vanguard. To do this, you have to learn how to discern the most important aspect of

---

1. As part of the reorganization of the Integrated Revolutionary Organizations (ORI) into the United Party of the Socialist Revolution (PURS) in 1962–63, a procedure was established whereby workers were nominated for the pool from which the party selects its members by their fellow workers at assemblies in their workplace. That procedure continues today in the Communist Party of Cuba.

things being stressed by the government, which represents the people and is, at the same time, a party.

Similarly, one must know how to weigh things and set priorities. These are tasks the youth organization must carry out.

You have been talking about the technological revolution. This is one of the most important things, one of the most concrete tasks and one that is closest to the mentality of youth. But one cannot seek to carry out a technological revolution by oneself, because the technological revolution is happening all over the world, in every country, both socialist and nonsocialist—I am referring to the advanced countries, of course.

There is a technological revolution going on in the United States. There's a powerful technological revolution in France, in Britain, in the Federal Republic of Germany, and these are certainly not socialist countries. So the technological revolution must have a class content, a socialist content. And for this to happen, there must be a transformation of the youth so that they become a genuine motor force. In other words, all the bad habits of the old, dead society must be eliminated. One cannot think about a technological revolution without at the same time thinking about a communist attitude toward work. This is extremely important. We cannot speak of a socialist technological revolution if there is not a communist attitude toward work.

This is simply the reflection in Cuba of the technological revolution taking place as a result of the most recent scientific inventions and discoveries. These are things that cannot be separated. And a communist attitude toward work consists of changes taking place in an individual's consciousness, changes that naturally take a long time. We cannot expect that changes of this sort will be completed within a short period, during which work will continue to have the character it has now—a compulsory social obligation—before being transformed into a social necessity. In other words, this transformation—the technological revolution—presents the opportunity to get closer to what interests you most in life, your work, your research, your studies of every type. And one's attitude toward this work will be something totally new. Work will be what Sunday is now—not the Sunday when you cut cane, but the Sunday when you don't cut cane. In other words, work will be seen as a necessity, not something compelled by sanctions.

But achieving that requires a long process, a process tied to the creation of habits acquired through voluntary work. Why do we emphasize voluntary work so much? Economically it means practically nothing. Even the volunteers who cut cane—which is the most important task from an economic point of view—don't accomplish much. A volunteer cutter from this ministry cuts only a fourth or a fifth of what a cane cutter who has been doing this his whole life does. It has economic importance today because of the shortage of labor. It is also important today because these individuals are giving a part of their lives to society without expecting anything in return, without expecting any kind of payment, simply fulfilling a duty to society. This is the first step in transforming work into what it will eventually become, as a result of the advance of technology, the advance of production, and the advance of the relations of production: an activity of a higher level, a social necessity.

We will advance if at every step we bring together the ability to transform ourselves, generalizing our attitude toward study of the new technology, with the ability to perform in our workplaces as the vanguard. And if you get into the habit of turning productive labor little by little into something that, over time, becomes a necessity, then you will automatically become the youth's vanguard, and you will never have to wonder what you should be doing. You will simply do what at the time seems to make the most sense. You won't have to go searching for what youth might like.

You will automatically be youth, as well as representatives of the most advanced youth. Those who are young, young in spirit especially, don't ever have to worry about what to do in order to please others. Just do what is necessary, what seems logical at the time. That's how youth will become leaders.

Today we have begun a process of, let us say, politicizing this ministry. The Ministry of Industry is really cold, a very bureaucratic place, a nest of nit-picking bureaucrats and bores, from the minister on down, who are constantly tackling concrete tasks in order to search for new relationships and new attitudes.

Now, the youth organization here was complaining that even though they had organized things, this place was empty on the days when I didn't show up, and they wanted me to raise this. Well, I can raise it, but I can't tell anyone to come here. What's going on? Either there is a lack of communication or a lack of interest, and this hasn't been overcome by the people in charge of doing so. This is a concrete task of the ministry. It is the task of the youth organization, to overcome the indifference within the ministry. Of course, there is always room for self-criticism; and the assessment that not enough has been done to stay in constant communication with people is always appropriate.

That's true, but it's also important that self-criticism be complete: because self-criticism is not self-flagellation but rather an analysis of a person's attitude. Moreover, the enormous amount of work on one's shoulders, one task after another all piled up, makes it more difficult to have a different type of relationship and to pursue a more human relationship, one could say, a relationship less directed through bureaucratic red tape.

This will come in due time: when work is not so urgent, when there are a whole number of cadres to lean on, when all tasks are always fulfilled, when lack of confidence in work done is no longer one of the disgraceful features of this entire stage of our revolution.

Today, it is necessary to check documents personally, double-check statistics personally, and errors are often still found. So once this stage has disappeared—and it is on the road to disappearing; it will soon disappear—when all the cadres are stronger, when each of us has advanced a little more, then of course there will be time for different types of relations. Naturally this doesn't mean a minister or a director going around asking everybody how their families are doing. Rather, we will be able to organize relations that enable us to work better both within the ministry and outside it, so we get to know each other better.

The aim of socialism today, in this current stage of building socialism and communism, is not simply to create shiny factories. These factories are being built for human beings in their totality. Man must be transformed in conjunction with advances in production. We would not be doing our job if we were solely producers of commodities, of raw material, and were not at the same time producers of men.

Here is one of the tasks of the youth: to give impetus to, and to lead through example, the production of the man of tomorrow. In this production and leadership, the production of oneself is included, because nobody is perfect, far from it. Everyone needs to be improving themselves through work, through relations with other people, through serious study, critical discussions—these are all things that contribute to the transformation of people. We know all this because five long years have passed since our revolution triumphed, and seven long years since the first of us landed and began the struggle, the final stage of the struggle. Whoever looks back and thinks about what he was like seven years ago will realize that we have traveled far, very far, but there is still a long way to go.

These are the tasks, and the most important thing is for the youth to understand their role and their fundamental task. They shouldn't inflate that role more than is merited. They should not consider themselves the center of the socialist universe. Rather, they should see themselves as an important link, a very important one that points toward the future.

We ourselves are already on the decline, even if geographically speaking we might still be situated among the youth. We have carried out many hard tasks, we have had the responsibility of leading a country through tremendously difficult times, and naturally all this ages us, it wears us out. Within a few years the task of those of us remaining will be to retire to winter quarters so that new generations can occupy our posts. In any case, I think we have played an important role, and have done so with a certain amount of dignity. But our job will not be complete unless we know the right time to step aside. And another task in front of you is to create the people who will replace us. That we can be forgotten as a thing of the past will become one of the most important gauges of the work carried out by the youth as a whole and by the entire people.

Che and his men
come as reinforcements

Fidel Castro pays tribute to Che and his comrades
October 17, 1997

In 1965 Che Guevara resigned his political, military, and other responsibilities. "Other nations of the world summon my modest efforts of assistance," he wrote in a letter of farewell to Fidel Castro. In October 1967 Guevara was killed in Bolivia while fighting to topple the U.S.-backed military dictatorship in that country and to link up with rising revolutionary struggles in his native Argentina and elsewhere in the Southern Cone of Latin America.

In the more than three decades since his death in combat, Guevara's communist political legacy has remained central to the course of the Cuban Revolution. His example continues to inspire millions of working people and youth both in Cuba and throughout the world.

In 1997 Guevara's remains, buried in great secrecy by the Bolivian regime, were uncovered there, together with those of six other revolutionary combatants from Bolivia, Cuba, and Peru who fought by his side. Their next of kin requested they be brought to Cuba, where hundreds of thousands of

Above: Fidel Castro addressing October 17, 1997, ceremony in Santa Clara where remains of Guevara and others who fought and died in Bolivia in 1967 were interred. Seated, General of the Army Raúl Castro, minister of the Revolutionary Armed Forces, and Carlos Lage, vice president of the Council of State. **Below**: Part of the assembled crowd of tens of thousands paying tribute.

"Che was truly a communist. Today he is an example, a model of what a revolutionary is, what a communist is."

Cuban workers and youth mobilized to pay tribute to the combatants and to express their determination to remain true to their revolutionary course.

The speech that follows was given by Cuban president Fidel Castro on October 17, at a solemn ceremony in Santa Clara, where the remains of the combatants were interred at the site of a monument dedicated to the memory of Ernesto Che Guevara.

~

Relatives of the comrades who died in battle; invited guests; residents of Villa Clara; compatriots: [*Applause*]

With deep emotion, we are living through one of those moments that is not often repeated.

We did not come to bid farewell to Che and his heroic comrades. We came to greet them.

I view Che and his men as reinforcements, as a detachment of invincible combatants that this time includes not just Cubans. It also includes Latin Americans who have come to fight at our side and to write new pages of history and glory.

I view Che, furthermore, as a moral giant who grows day by day, whose image, whose strength, whose influence has multiplied throughout the world.

How could he fit below a tombstone?

How could he fit in this plaza?

How could he fit solely in our beloved but small island?

Only the world he dreamed of, which he lived and fought for, is big enough for him.

The more that injustice, exploitation, inequality, unemployment, poverty, hunger, and misery prevail in human society, the more Che's stature will grow.

The more that the power of imperialism, hegemonism, domination, and interventionism grow, to the detriment of the most sacred rights of the peoples—especially the weak, backward, and poor peoples who for centuries were colonies of the West and sources of slave labor—the more the values Che defended will be upheld.

The more that abuses, selfishness, and alienation exist; the more that Indians, ethnic minorities, women, and immigrants suffer discrimination; the more that children are bought and sold for sex or forced into the workforce in their hundreds of millions; the more that ignorance, unsanitary conditions, insecurity, and homelessness prevail—the more Che's deeply humanistic message will stand out.

The more that corrupt, demagogic, and hypocritical politicians exist anywhere, the more Che's example of a pure, revolutionary, and consistent human being will come through.

The more cowards, opportunists, and traitors there are on the face of the earth, the more Che's personal courage and revolutionary integrity will be admired. The more that others lack the ability to fulfill their duty, the more Che's iron willpower will be admired. The more that some individuals lack the most basic self-respect, the more Che's sense of honor and dignity will be admired. The more that skeptics abound, the more Che's faith in man will be admired. The more pessimists there are, the more Che's optimism will be admired. The more vacillators there are, the more Che's audacity will be admired. The more that loafers squander the product of the labor of others, the more Che's austerity, his spirit of study and work, will be admired.

Che was truly a communist and today he is an example and a model of what a revolutionary is and what a communist is.

Che was a teacher and forger of human beings like himself. Consistent in his actions, he always practiced what he preached, and he always demanded more of himself than of others.

Whenever a volunteer was needed for a difficult mission, Che would be the first to step forward, both in wartime and in peacetime. He always subordinated his great dreams to his readiness to generously give his life. Nothing was impossible for him, and he was capable of making the impossible possible.

Among other actions, the invasion from the Sierra Maestra westward through immense and unprotected plains, and the capture of the city of Santa Clara with just a few men, testify to the feats he was capable of.[1]

His ideas concerning revolution in his country of origin and the rest of South America were possible, despite enormous difficulties. Had they been achieved, perhaps the world today would be different. Vietnam proved that it was possible to fight the interventionist forces of imperialism and defeat them. The Sandinistas [in Nicaragua] defeated one of the most powerful puppets of the United States. The Salvadoran revolutionaries were on the verge of attaining victory. In Africa, apartheid was defeated despite the nuclear weapons it possessed. China, thanks to the heroic struggle of its workers and peasants, is one of the countries with the greatest prospects in the world. Hong Kong had to be returned after 150 years of occupation, originally carried out to impose the drug trade on an immense country.

Different epochs and different circumstances do not require identical methods and identical tactics. But nothing can stop the course of history; its objective laws have

---

1. See page 36.

enduring value. Che based himself on those laws and had absolute faith in human beings. Often humanity's great revolutionaries, those responsible for great transformations, did not have the privilege of seeing their dreams realized as quickly as they hoped or desired, but sooner or later they have triumphed.

A combatant may die, but not his ideas.

What was an agent of the U.S. government doing there, where Che was wounded and held captive?[2] Why did they believe that by killing him he would cease to exist as a combatant? Today he is not in La Higuera. Instead, he is everywhere; he is to be found wherever there is a just cause to defend. Those with a stake in eliminating him and making him disappear were incapable of understanding that he had already left an indelible mark on history; that his shining, prophetic vision would become a symbol for all the poor of this world, in their millions. Young people, children, the elderly, men and women who knew him, honest persons throughout the world, regardless of their social origin, admire him.

Che is waging and winning more battles than ever.

Thank you Che, for your personal history, your life, and your example.

Thank you for coming to reinforce us in this difficult struggle we are waging today to save the ideas you fought so hard for, to save the revolution, the homeland, and the conquests of socialism, which is a realization of part of the great dreams you held so dear! [*Applause*] We are counting on you to help us carry out this enormous feat, to defeat the imperialist plans against Cuba, to resist the

---

2. An agent of the CIA, Félix Rodríguez, accompanied Guevara's captors and helped direct his execution by the Bolivian army in the town of La Higuera.

blockade, to achieve victory. [*Applause*]

As you can see, this land, which is your land; this people, which is your people; this revolution, which is your revolution, continues upholding with honor and pride the banners of socialism. [*Applause*]

Welcome, heroic comrades from the reinforcement detachment. The enemy will never be able to conquer the trench of ideas and the trench of justice that you will be defending alongside our people! And together we will continue fighting for a better world!

Hasta la victoria siempre! [Ever onward to victory] [*Ovation*]

GLOSSARY NOTES

Agrarian Reform Law – Enacted by the revolutionary government May 17, 1959, it set a limit of 30 caballerías (approximately 1,000 acres) on individual landholdings. Implementation of the law resulted in the confiscation of the vast estates in Cuba—many of them owned by wealthy U.S. families and corporations. These lands passed into the hands of the new government. The law also granted sharecroppers, tenant farmers, and squatters title to the land they tilled. Some 100,000 peasant families received deeds.

A provision of the law created the National Institute of Agrarian Reform (INRA) as the instrument for its implementation. INRA was granted sweeping powers over virtually every aspect of the economy. Under the leadership of the cadres of the Rebel Army and the July 26 Movement it became the central government body that mobilized workers and peasants to defend their interests.

A second agrarian reform in 1963 confiscated landholdings in excess of 165 acres. This law affected 10,000 capitalist farmers who still owned 20 percent of Cuba's agricultural land and brought property relations on the land in line with those already established through the nationalizations of industry in the latter half of 1960.

Albizu Campos, Pedro (1891 1965) – Leader of the Puerto Rican Nationalist Party. Jailed or placed under house arrest for a total of nearly a quarter century by the U.S. government for proindependence activities, 1937–47, 1950–53, and 1954–64.

Paralyzed by a stroke in 1956, he was released from prison just prior to his death.

Arbenz, Jacobo (1914–1971) – Elected president of Guatemala in 1951, he was overthrown by a U.S.-backed coup in 1954.

Association of Rebel Youth (AJR). See Union of Young Communists.

Batista, Fulgencio (1901–1973) – As a result of the popular revolution of August 1933 that toppled the dictatorship of Gerardo Machado, a movement arose within the Cuban army of noncommissioned officers and soldiers against the old Machadista officer corps. Fulgencio Batista, a sergeant and stenographer, was one of its leaders. Batista became army chief of staff and, with the support of the U.S. embassy, emerged as the strongman of the regime, unleashing a reign of terror against popular organizations. The revolutionary upsurge was suppressed and Batista remained in power until 1944, when he left office, retaining a base within the army officer corps.

On March 10, 1952, Batista organized a military coup against the government headed by Authentic Party leader Carlos Prío and canceled impending elections. With support from Washington, Batista imposed an increasingly brutal military dictatorship that lasted until January 1, 1959. On that day, as his military and police forces began surrendering to the victorious Rebel Army advancing under the command of Fidel Castro, and as a general strike and popular insurrection spread, Batista fled the country.

Bay of Pigs – On April 17, 1961, an expeditionary force of 1,500 Cuban mercenaries invaded Cuba at the Bay of Pigs on the southern coast. The counterrevolutionaries, organized and financed by Washington, aimed to hold a beachhead long enough to install on Cuban territory a provisional government already formed in the United States that would appeal for Washington's support and direct military intervention. The mercenaries, however, were defeated within seventy-two hours by Cuba's militia and Revolutionary Armed Forces. On April 19 the remaining invaders were captured at Playa Girón (Girón Beach), which is the name Cubans use to designate the battle.

Ben Bella, Ahmed (b. 1918) – Leader of the National Liberation Front (FLN) of Algeria, which mobilized the Algerian people in the 1954–62 struggle for independence from France. Ben Bella was the president of the workers and farmers government that came to power following the victory over Paris in 1962 and collaborated closely with the Cuban government to advance anti-imperialist struggles in Africa and Latin America. He was overthrown in a coup led by Col. Houari Boumedienne in June 1965.

Betancourt, Rómulo (1908–1981) – President of Venezuela 1945–48 and 1958–64 and leader of the liberal Democratic Action party.

Blest, Clotario (1899–1990) – A longtime leader of the Chilean labor movement, president of the United Federation of Workers of Chile (CUTCH), and a supporter of the Cuban Revolution.

Bolívar, Simón (1783–1830) – Known as the Liberator. Latin American patriot, born in Caracas. He led an armed rebellion that helped win independence from Spain for much of Latin America.

Boti, Regino, Jr. (1923–1999) – Born in Guantánamo, Cuba, he studied first at the University of Havana, where he received a degree in civil law, and later at Harvard University, where he received a degree in economics, finance, and banking. He later went to work for the United Nations Economic Commission for Latin America. During Cuba's revolutionary war he became a collaborator of the July 26 Movement. He served as Cuba's minister of the economy from 1959 until 1964.

Castillo Armas, Carlos (1914–1957) – A colonel in the Guatemalan armed forces, he was installed as dictator by the U.S.-backed coup that toppled the government of Jacobo Arbenz in 1954. He was assassinated in 1957.

Castro Ruz, Fidel (b. 1926) – Born and raised in Oriente province in eastern Cuba. A student leader at the University of Havana beginning in 1945. Founding member of the Orthodox Party in 1947 and central organizer of its revolutionary-minded youth. One of the party's candidates for House of Representatives in the 1952 elections, which were canceled following the Batista coup. Castro led the July 26, 1953, attack on the Moncada and Bayamo garrisons that opened the revolutionary struggle against the dictatorship, and was sentenced to fifteen years in prison. His courtroom defense speech, "History Will Absolve Me," which he wrote down and smuggled out of prison, was distributed in tens of thousands of copies across Cuba, becoming the program of the revolutionary movement to oust the Batista regime. Released in May 1955 after a mass amnesty campaign, he led the founding of the July 26 Revolutionary Movement a few weeks later.

In Mexico, Castro prepared the expeditionary force that, aboard the yacht *Granma,* returned to Cuba in December 1956. From the Sierra Maestra mountains, he commanded the Rebel Army during the 1956–58 revolutionary war. In May 1958 he became general secretary of the July 26 Movement.

Castro was Cuba's prime minister from February 1959 to 1976, when he was elected president of the Council of State and of the Council of Ministers. He is commander in chief of the armed forces and has been first secretary of the Communist Party of Cuba since it was founded in 1965.

Castro Ruz, Raúl (b. 1931) – Born and raised in Oriente province in eastern Cuba. A student leader at the University of Havana, he participated in the 1953 Moncada attack and was sentenced to thirteen years in prison. He was released in May 1955 following a national amnesty campaign. A founding member of the July 26 Movement, he was a participant in the *Granma* expedition. In February 1958 he was promoted to commander and headed the Second Eastern Front.

Since October 1959 he has been minister of the Revolutionary Armed Forces. He was vice premier from 1959 to 1976, when he was elected first vice president of the Council of State and of the Council of Ministers. Since 1965 he has been second secretary of the Communist Party of Cuba. He holds the rank of general of the army, the second-highest officer in the Revolutionary Armed Forces after Commander in Chief Fidel Castro.

Cienfuegos, Camilo (1932–1959) – A *Granma* expeditionary, he became a Rebel Army commander in 1958. From August to October 1958 he led a column westward from the Sierra Maestra en route to Pinar del Río. He operated in northern Las Villas province until the end of the war, working in tandem with the column led by Che Guevara based in the southern part of the province. He was named head of the Rebel Army following the victory over Batista in January 1959. His small Cessna 310 was lost at sea in October 1959 while he was returning to Havana from a mission in Camagüey to combat a counterrevolutionary mutiny led by Huber Matos.

Committees for the Defense of the Revolution (CDRs) – Launched in September 1960 on a block-by-block basis as a tool through which the Cuban people could exercise vigilance against counterrevolutionary activity. In subsequent years they have also served as a vehicle to organize participation at mass demonstrations and to take part in vaccination and other public health campaigns, civil defense, the fight against petty crime, and other civic tasks.

Communist Party of Cuba – In 1961, the July 26 Revolutionary Movement initiated a process of fusion with the Popular Socialist Party and the Revolutionary Directorate—all three of which had experienced defections and a regroupment of forces as the revolution deepened. In 1961 the Integrated Revolutionary Organizations (ORI) was created. In 1963 the United Party of the Socialist Revolution (PURS) was formed from the ORI; and in October 1965 the Communist Party of Cuba was founded, with Fidel Castro first secretary of its Central Committee.

Diario de la Marina – A reactionary Cuban daily founded in 1832, closely tied to Spanish colonialism and the Catholic church hierarchy. It became an organizing center for the counterrevolution and was closed by the revolutionary government May 13, 1960.

Díaz Lanz, Pedro Luis – Head of the Cuban air force January–June 1959, he fled to the United States June 29, 1959. He conducted an air raid on Havana October 21, 1959.

Dorticós, Osvaldo (1919–1983) – Regional coordinator of the July 26 Movement in Cienfuegos and dean of the Cienfuegos law school, he was forced into exile in December 1958. In July 1959 he became president of Cuba, holding that position until 1976. He was a member of the Communist Party Central Committee and Political Bureau at the time of his death.

Dulles, Allen (1893–1969) – Director of the U.S. Central Intelligence Agency, 1953–61, he oversaw Washington's covert operations— including large-scale terrorist actions, assassinations, coup d'états and attempted coups—in Guatemala, Iran, the Congo, Cuba, and elsewhere. He resigned in the wake of the U.S. government fiasco at the Bay of Pigs. Brother of John Foster Dulles.

Dulles, John Foster (1888–1959) – U.S. secretary of state 1953–59 in the administration of Dwight D. Eisenhower. He had been a long-time attorney for and stockholder in the United Fruit Company (today United Brands).

Fierro, Martín – The protagonist of an epic poem by late nineteenth-century Argentine writer José Hernández that recounts the life of the gauchos (cowboys) of the Argentine pampas and protests the discrimination and exploitation to which they were subjected.

Granma – The yacht that carried eighty-two revolutionary fighters commanded by Fidel Castro from Tuxpan, Mexico, to Cuba to initiate the revolutionary war against the U.S.-backed regime of Fulgencio Batista. The expeditionaries landed in southeast Cuba on December 2, 1956. *Granma* has been the name of the daily newspaper of the Communist Party of Cuba since 1965.

Guatemala coup, 1954 – Seeking to crush broadening political and social struggles in Guatemala accompanying a land reform initiated by the regime of Jacobo Arbenz that affected the substantial holdings of United Fruit and other U.S. corporations, mercenary forces backed by Washington invaded the country in 1954. Arbenz refused to arm those ready to resist and resigned. A right-wing military dictatorship took over. Among those volunteering to fight the imperialist-organized attack was Ernesto Guevara, a young doctor who had been drawn to Guatemala by his support for the struggle unfolding there.

Guillén, Nicolás (1902–1989) – Cuban poet and a member of the National Committee of the Popular Socialist Party before the revolution. Persecuted by the dictatorship, he lived in exile during the revolutionary war, returning to Cuba in 1959. He became president of the Union of Writers and Artists in 1961 and was a member of the Communist Party Central Committee at the time of his death.

Hart, Armando (b. 1930) – Joined the Orthodox Youth in 1947 in Havana. He was a leader of the Revolutionary National Movement following Batista's coup. In 1955 he became a founding member of the July 26 Movement and a leader of its urban underground. He was imprisoned briefly in 1957 and escaped. He served as national coordinator of the July 26 Movement from early 1957 to January 1958, when he was captured and imprisoned on the Isle of Pines until January 1, 1959. He served as minister of education 1959–65; Communist Party organization secretary 1965–70; minister of culture 1976–97. He has been a member of the Communist Party Central Committee since 1965 and was a member of the Political Bureau 1965–86.

Iglesias, Joel (b. 1941) – Born into a peasant family on the outskirts of Santiago de Cuba, he joined the Rebel Army in 1957, serving in Columns 4 and 8 under Che Guevara; he was promoted to commander at the end of the revolutionary war. He became the first president of the Association of Rebel Youth, initiated by the Rebel Army Department of Instruction, in 1960, and general secretary of the UJC in 1962. He was a member of the Communist Party Central Committee 1965–75.

INRA. See Agrarian Reform Law.

July 26 Revolutionary Movement – Founded June 1955 by Fidel Castro and other participants in the attack on the Moncada garrison in Santiago de Cuba and the Carlos Manuel de Céspedes garrison in Bayamo, youth activists from the left wing of the Orthodox Party, and other revolutionary forces; it separated from the Orthodox Party in March 1956. During the revolutionary war it was composed of the Rebel Army in the mountains (*Sierra*) and the urban underground network (*Llano*), as well as revolutionists in exile. In May 1958 Fidel Castro became its general secretary. It published the newspaper *Revolución*, beginning in clandestinity.

In 1961 the July 26 Revolutionary Movement initiated a process of fusion with the Popular Socialist Party and the March 13 Revolutionary Directorate that led in 1965 to the founding of the Communist Party of Cuba, with Fidel Castro elected as its first secretary.

Lenin, V.I. (1870–1924) – Continuator in the imperialist epoch of the theoretical and practical work of Karl Marx and Frederick Engels, he was the central leader of the 1917 October Revolution in Russia. Founder of the Bolshevik Party. He was chair of the Council of People's Commissars (Soviet government) 1917–24 and a member of the Executive Committee of the Communist International.

Literacy Campaign – From late 1960 through 1961, the revolutionary government undertook a literacy drive to teach one million Cubans to read and write. Central to this effort was the mobilization of 100,000 young people to go to the countryside, where they lived with peasants and workers whom they were teaching. As a result of this drive, Cuba virtually eliminated illiteracy. During the literacy campaign nine participants, both students and teachers, were murdered by counterrevolutionaries, organized, armed, and financed by Washington.

Lumumba, Patrice (1925–1961) – Leader of the independence struggle in the Congo and its prime minister after independence from Belgium in June 1960. In September 1960, after requesting United Nations troops to counter attacks by Belgian-organized mercenaries, his government was overthrown in a U.S.-backed coup. UN troops supposedly protecting Lumumba took no action as he was captured, jailed, and then murdered in January 1961 by Congolese forces collaborating with Washington. A U.S. Senate investigating committee in 1975 concluded that CIA chief Allen Dulles ordered the assassination; moreover, there was a "reasonable inference" that the order originated with President Dwight D. Eisenhower.

Malcolm X (1925–1965) – One of the most outstanding proletarian revolutionists in U.S. history. Born into a working-class family, he was imprisoned as a young man. While in prison, seeking a way to get back on his feet, he joined the Nation of Islam (NOI) and, after his release in 1952, became a leader of that organization. A supporter of the Cuban Revolution, as the NOI leader in Harlem he greeted Fidel Castro in September 1960 when Castro stayed there during a visit to New York to speak before the United Nations. Repelled by the discovery of corrupt and hypocritical political conduct in the top leadership of the Nation of Islam, he broke from the NOI in early 1964. He formed the Organization of Afro-American Unity later that year open to all Blacks who sought to mount a united struggle against racist inequality and social injustice and to forge alliances with all those committed to the revolutionary internationalist goals he was advancing. During the last year of his life, he developed increasingly anticapitalist and prosocialist views. He was assassinated in New York City on February 21, 1965.

Mao Zedong (1893–1976) – Chairman of the Chinese Communist Party from 1935, he was the central leader of the Third Chinese Revolution and headed the People's Republic of China from 1949 until his death.

Mariátegui, José Carlos (1895–1930) – Peruvian writer who, under the impact of the Russian Revolution, was attracted to Marxism while living in Europe 1919–23. After his return to Peru he founded the magazine *Amauta*. In 1928 Mariátegui helped found the Socialist Party of Peru, which had ties to the Communist International but did not seek formal affiliation. Mariátegui became its general secretary. That same year he laid the groundwork for the establishment of the country's first trade union federation, the General Confederation of Peruvian Workers. In 1929 the Socialist Party's delegation to the Communist International's First Conference of Latin American Communist Parties held in Buenos Aires was sharply criticized by representatives of the Communist International and leaders of Communist Parties in Latin America for, among other things, not calling themselves Communist and placing themselves under the discipline of the Comintern. Mariátegui died before the issue was resolved. After his death the majority of the Socialist Party became the Communist Party of Peru. Mariátegui's actions and writings, like those of his Cuban contemporary Julio Antonio Mella, have had an impact on the revolutionary movement in Latin America beyond the borders of his own country.

Martí, José (1853–1895) – A noted revolutionary, poet, writer, speaker, and journalist, he is Cuba's national hero. He founded the Cuban Revolutionary Party in 1892 to fight Spanish rule and oppose U.S. designs on Cuba. He organized and planned the

1895 independence war and was killed in battle at Dos Ríos in Oriente province. His revolutionary anti-imperialist program is part of the internationalist traditions and political heritage of the Cuban Revolution.

Marx, Karl (1818–1883) – Founder with Frederick Engels (1820–1895) of the modern communist workers movement; architect of its theoretical foundations.

Matos, Huber (b. 1918) – A small landowner in Oriente province, he joined the Rebel Army in March 1958, becoming commander of Column no. 9 of the Third Front led by Juan Almeida. As military head of Camagüey province in October 1959, he was arrested for an attempted counterrevolutionary mutiny and was imprisoned until 1979. Currently living in the United States, he heads the counterrevolutionary Cuba Independent and Democratic.

Medrano, Humberto – Assistant director of *Prensa Libre* newspaper in Havana 1949–60. He opposed the revolutionary government's measures and left Cuba via the Panamanian embassy in May 1960. For many years he has worked for the U.S. government's Radio and TV Martí.

Mella, Julio Antonio (1903–1929) – President of the Federation of University Students (FEU) and leader of the university reform movement in Cuba in 1923. He was a founding leader of the Communist Party of Cuba in 1925. Arrested by the police of the Machado dictatorship, he escaped to Mexico in 1926, where he organized against the dictatorship and joined in the international campaigns to defend Sacco and Vanzetti, Augusto César Sandino, and others. In 1927 he attended the Brussels congress of the Anti-Imperialist League, then traveled to Moscow. Hounded by Machado's agents, he was assassinated on a Mexico City street in January 1929. Mella, Camilo Cienfuegos, and Ernesto Che Guevara are the three examples for Cuban youth today represented on the emblem of the Union of Young Communists (UJC) in Cuba.

Mikoyan, Anastas (1895–1978) – Joined the Bolshevik Party in 1915. Prominent in the officialdom of the Soviet Communist Party under Stalin, he was first deputy premier of the Soviet government between 1955 and 1964 with responsibility for directing the country's foreign trade.

Miró Cardona, José (1902–1974) – A leader of the bourgeois opposition to Batista and president of the Cuban Bar Association, he was prime minister of Cuba, January–February 1959, replaced by Fidel Castro. In 1960 he left Cuba for the United States, where he served as president of the counterrevolutionary organization known as the Revolutionary Democratic Front, and later of the Cuban Revolutionary Council in exile. He later moved to Puerto Rico.

Moncada garrison – On July 26, 1953, some 160 combatants, overwhelmingly youth, under the command of Fidel Castro launched an insurrectionary attack on the Moncada army garrison in Santiago de Cuba together with a simultaneous one on the garrison in Bayamo, opening the revolutionary armed struggle against the Batista dictatorship. After the attack's failure, Batista's forces massacred more than fifty of the captured revolutionaries. Fidel Castro and twenty-seven others, including Raúl Castro and Juan Almeida, were tried and sentenced to up to fifteen years in prison. They were released on May 15, 1955, after a public defense campaign forced Batista's regime to issue an amnesty.

Organization of American States (OAS) – Created in 1948 under the tutelage of the U.S. government, this body, composed of most countries of the Americas, has been an instrument to advance Washington's interests. At an OAS ministerial meeting in Punta del Este, Uruguay, in 1961, Washington presented a plan for U.S. "economic assistance" to Latin America called the Alliance for Progress. Cuba's representative at that meeting, Ernesto Che Guevara, exposed the exploitative nature of this program, and its purpose as a weapon to counter the appeal of the Cuban Revolution to millions throughout the Americas. In 1962 the OAS expelled Cuba, claiming it was promoting subversion throughout Latin America. The organization soon endorsed the U.S. economic measures to strangle Cuba and other acts of aggression against the revolution.

ORI (Integrated Revolutionary Organizations). See Communist Party of Cuba.

País, Frank (1934–1957) – Vice president of the Federation of University Students in Oriente, he was the central leader of Oriente Revolutionary Action, later renamed Revolutionary National Action, which fused with the Moncada veterans and other forces to form the July 26 Movement in 1955. He was the central leader of the July 26 Movement in Oriente province, national action coordinator of the July 26 Movement, and head of its urban militias. He was murdered by the dictatorship's forces July 30, 1957.

Pérez Jiménez, Marcos (b. 1914) – Chief of the Venezuelan army's general staff, he led a military coup in 1948 that installed a three-man junta. He proclaimed himself president in 1952 and was ousted in 1958 by a popular uprising.

Platt Amendment – Named after U.S. Senator Orville Platt, the Platt Amendment was a provision imposed on the Cuban government that was established during the U.S. military occupation following 1898. Under the terms of that amendment—incorporated in Cuba's new constitution—Washington was given the "right" to intervene in Cuban affairs at any time and to establish military bases on Cuban soil. The Platt Amendment was eliminated from the Cuban constitution in the wake of the 1933–34 revolutionary upsurge there, but Washington maintained its naval base in Guantánamo, granted in virtual perpetuity during the U.S. occupation, as well as other forms of political and economic domination such as the reciprocal trade treaty.

Playa Girón. See Bay of Pigs.

Popular Socialist Party (PSP) – Name taken in 1944 by the Communist Party of Cuba founded in 1925. The PSP actively opposed the 1952 Batista coup and dictatorship but rejected the political course of the Moncada assault and of the July 26 Movement and Rebel Army in launching the revolutionary war in 1956–57. The PSP participated in the campaign to save the life of Fidel Castro and the other survivors of the Moncada attack and joined the nationwide amnesty effort that won their release from prison. The PSP collaborated with the Rebel Army, and in 1958 joined the armed insurrection to topple the Batista dictatorship. As the revolution deepened following the 1959 victory, the PSP, like the July 26 Movement and Revolutionary Directorate, went through a process of political differentiation. In mid 1961 the Integrated Revolutionary Organizations (ORI) was formed by a fusion of the three groups, initiating a process that led in 1965 to the founding of the Communist Party of Cuba.

Prensa Libre – Capitalist newspaper published in Havana. An organizing center for the counterrevolution, it was closed by the revolutionary government May 16, 1960.

Quevedo, Angel – A lieutenant in the Revolutionary Directorate military column during the anti-Batista struggle, he was promoted to commander in the Rebel Army in 1959. He was a student at the University of Havana that year and was president of the Commission for the Complete Reform of the University. He later became general secretary of the Federation of University Students.

Quevedo, Miguel Angel (d. 1969) – Editor of the magazine *Bohemia* prior to fleeing to the United States July 18, 1960.

Rebel Army – Began military operations against the Batista regime December 2, 1956, when the *Granma* landed in Oriente province. Its defeat of the Batista army forces in numerous decisive engagements, especially from July 1958 on, gave impetus to a revolutionary upsurge throughout Cuba and sealed the fate of the dictatorship. Rebel Army cadres became the backbone of the new revolutionary institutions that emerged, including the Revolutionary Armed Forces, the National Institute of Agrarian Reform, the militias, the police, the Association of Rebel Youth, and by October 1959, the large majority of government ministers.

Revolutionary Directorate, March 13 – Organization formed in 1955 by José Antonio Echeverría and other leaders of the Federation of University Students in the struggle against Batista. It organized an attack on Batista's Presidential Palace on March 13, 1957, in which a number of central leaders, including Echeverría, were killed. It organized a guerrilla column in the Escambray mountains in Las Villas in February 1958 led by Faure Chomón that fought under the command of Che Guevara in the last months of the revolutionary war. In 1961 it fused with the July 26 Movement and PSP in a process that eventually led to the founding of the Communist Party of Cuba in 1965.

Rivero, José Ignacio "Pepín" (b. 1920) – Director of the right-wing newspaper *Diario de la Marina* 1947–60. An opponent of the Cuban Revolution; he took asylum in Vatican offices in Cuba May 10, 1960.

Sanguily, Manuel (1848–1925) – Veteran of the Cuban independence war of 1868–78. He later served in the U.S.-dominated Cuban government, where he opposed the Platt Amendment and other designs by Washington on Cuba.

Sierra Maestra – Located in southeastern Cuba, the Sierra Maestra is the highest mountain range in Cuba. During Cuba's revolutionary war of 1956–58 it was the base of the Rebel Army led by Fidel Castro.

Turquino – Located in the Sierra Maestra, Turquino is the highest mountain in Cuba.

Union of Young Communists (UJC) – Born out of the Association of Rebel Youth (AJR) founded by the Rebel Army Department of Instruction in December 1959. Following a fusion of pro-revolutionary youth organizations in October 1960, the AJR encompassed youth from the July 26 Movement, March 13 Revolutionary Directorate, and the Popular Socialist Party's Socialist Youth. It adopted the name UJC on April 4, 1962.

Ydígoras, Miguel (1895–1982) – Guatemalan president from 1958 to 1963, when he was ousted by a coup. An avowed enemy of the Cuban Revolution.

FOR FURTHER READING

Throughout Che Guevara Talks to Young People, *readers will come across references to historical events, speeches, and individuals that may be unfamiliar. The following are suggestions for further reading.*

Castro, Fidel, "The Case of Cuba Is the Case of All Underdeveloped Countries," Speech to the General Assembly of the United Nations, September 26, 1960. In *To Speak the Truth: Why Washington's 'Cold War' against Cuba Doesn't End* (Pathfinder, 1992).

Castro, Fidel, "History Will Absolve Me," Castro's 1953 courtroom defense speech explaining the political and social goals of the revolutionary struggle in Cuba initiated by the attack on the Moncada garrison. In *Fidel Castro's Political Strategy* (Pathfinder, 1987).

Castro, Fidel, "Against Bureaucracy and Sectarianism," March 26, 1962, televised speech explaining the correction of practices in the functioning of the Integrated Revolutionary Organizations (ORI) that, if allowed to continue, would have alienated broad layers of peasants and workers from the party. In *Selected Speeches of Fidel Castro* (Pathfinder, 1979).

Guevara, Ernesto Che, *Socialism and Man in Cuba* (Pathfinder, 1989).

Guevara, Ernesto Che, *Episodes of the Cuban Revolutionary War, 1956–58* (Pathfinder, 1996).

Guevara, Ernesto Che, "At the Afro-Asian Conference," February 24, 1965, speech to a meeting of the Organization of Afro-Asian Solidarity in Algiers. In *Che Guevara Speaks* (Pathfinder, 1967).

Guevara, Ernesto Che, "Voluntary Work Is a School for Communist Consciousness," a speech given August 15, 1964, and "Planning and Consciousness in the Transition to Socialism ('On the Budgetary Finance System')." In *Che Guevara and the Cuban Revolution: Writings and Speeches of Ernesto Che Guevara* (Pathfinder, 1987).

Guevara, Ernesto Che, "On the Concept of Value" and "The Meaning of Socialist Planning." In *New International* no. 8.

Lenin, V.I., writings and speeches on the national and colonial question. In *Workers of the World and Oppressed Peoples, Unite! Proceedings and Documents of the Second Congress of the Communist International, 1920* (Pathfinder, 1991); and *To See the Dawn, Baku 1920: First Congress of the Peoples of the East* (Pathfinder, 1993).

Lenin, V.I., *Lenin's Final Fight: Speeches and Writings, 1922–23* (Pathfinder, 1995).

Marx, Karl, *Critique of the Gotha Program* (International Publishers, 1966).

Marx, Karl, "Theses on Feuerbach," and **Engels, Frederick,** *Ludwig Feuerbach and the End of Classical German Philosophy.* In *Selected Works of Marx and Engels* (Lawrence & Wishart, 1991).

The Second Declaration of Havana *with* **The First Declaration of Havana.** The September 1960 First Declaration of Havana was issued in response to the Declaration of San José, Costa Rica—the U.S. government-engineered condemnation of revolutionary Cuba by the Organization of American States. The February 1962 Second Declaration of Havana is a call for revolutionary struggle by workers and peasants across the Americas. Each declaration was approved by acclamation at a rally of more than one million in Havana (Pathfinder, 1994).

INDEX

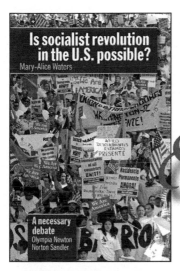

Is Socialist Revolution in the U.S. Possible?

A Necessary Debate

MARY-ALICE WATERS

Not only is socialist revolution in the U.S. possible, says Waters. Revolutionary struggles by working people are *inevitable*—initiated not by the toilers, but by the crisis-driven assaults of the propertied classes. As a fighting vanguard of the working class emerges in the U.S., the outlines of these coming battles— whose outcome is *not* inevitable—can already be seen. The future depends on us. $5. Also in Spanish and French.

Cuba and the Coming American Revolution

JACK BARNES

The Cuban Revolution of 1959 had a worldwide political impact, including on working people and youth in the imperialist heartland. As the mass, proletarian-based struggle for Black rights was already advancing in the U.S., the social transformation fought for and won by the Cuban toilers set an example that socialist revolution is not only necessary—it can be made and defended. This second edition, with a new foreword by Mary-Alice Waters, should be read alongside *Is Socialist Revolution in the U.S. Possible?* $10. Also in Spanish and French.

Revolutionary Continuity

Marxist Leadership in the U.S.

FARRELL DOBBS

How successive generations of fighters joined in the struggles that shaped the U.S. labor movement, seeking to build a class-conscious revolutionary leadership capable of advancing the interests of workers and small farmers and linking up with fellow toilers worldwide. 2 vols. *The Early Years: 1848–1917,* $20; *Birth of the Communist Movement: 1918–1922,* $19.

www.pathfinderpress.com

The First and Second Declarations of Havana

Nowhere are the questions of revolutionary strategy that today confront men and women on the front lines of struggles in the Americas addressed with greater truthfulness and clarity than in these uncompromising indictments of imperialist plunder and "the exploitation of man by man." Adopted by million-strong assemblies of the Cuban people in 1960 and 1962. $10. Also in Spanish and French.

Our History Is Still Being Written

The Story of Three Chinese–Cuban Generals in the Cuban Revolution

Armando Choy, Gustavo Chui, and Moisés Sío Wong talk about the historic place of Chinese immigration to Cuba, as well as over five decades of revolutionary action and internationalism, from Cuba to Angola and Venezuela today. Through their stories we see the social and political forces that gave birth to the Cuban nation and opened the door to socialist revolution in the Americas. $20. Also in Spanish.

To Speak the Truth

Why Washington's 'Cold War' against Cuba Doesn't End

FIDEL CASTRO, ERNESTO CHE GUEVARA

In historic speeches before the United Nations and UN bodies, Guevara and Castro address the peoples of the world, explaining why the U.S. government so fears the example set by the socialist revolution in Cuba and why Washington's effort to destroy it will fail. $17

www.pathfinderpress.com

Episodes of the Cuban Revolutionary War, 1956–58

ERNESTO CHE GUEVARA

A firsthand account of the political events and military campaigns that culminated in the January 1959 popular insurrection that overthrew the U.S.-backed dictatorship in Cuba. With clarity and humor, Guevara describes his own political education. He explains how the struggle transformed the men and women of the Rebel Army and July 26 Movement, opening the door to the first socialist revolution in the Americas. $30. Also in Spanish.

From the Escambray to the Congo

In the Whirlwind of the Cuban Revolution

VÍCTOR DREKE

The author describes how easy it became after the Cuban Revolution to take down a rope segregating blacks from whites in the town square, yet how enormous was the battle to transform social relations underlying all the "ropes" inherited from capitalism and Yankee domination. Dreke, second in command of the internationalist column in the Congo led by Che Guevara in 1965, recounts the creative joy with which working people have defended their revolutionary course—from Cuba's Escambray mountains to Africa and beyond. $17. Also in Spanish.

Playa Girón/Bay of Pigs

Washington's First Military Defeat in the Americas

FIDEL CASTRO, JOSÉ RAMÓN FERNÁNDEZ

In fewer than 72 hours of combat in April 1961, Cuba's revolutionary armed forces defeated a U.S.-organized invasion by 1,500 mercenaries. In the process, the Cuban people set an example for workers, farmers, and youth the world over that with political consciousness, class solidarity, courage, and revolutionary leadership, one can stand up to enormous might and seemingly insurmountable odds—and win. $20. Also in Spanish.

Dynamics of the Cuban Revolution

A Marxist Appreciation

JOSEPH HANSEN

How did the Cuban Revolution unfold? Why does it represent an "unbearable challenge" to U.S. imperialism? What political obstacles has it overcome? Written as the revolution advanced from its earliest days. $25

REVOLUTIONARY LEADERS IN THEIR OWN WORDS

MALCOLM X TALKS TO YOUNG PEOPLE

Four talks and an interview given to young people in Ghana, the United Kingdom, and the United States in the last months of Malcolm's life. This new edition contains the entire December 1964 presentation by Malcolm X at the Oxford University in the United Kingdom, in print for the first time anywhere. The collection concludes with two memorial tributes by a young socialist leader to this great revolutionary. $15. Also in Spanish.

CHE GUEVARA SPEAKS

SELECTED SPEECHES AND WRITINGS

"A faithful reflection of Che as he was, or, better, as he developed"—from the preface by Joseph Hansen. In twenty speeches, interviews, and letters, Guevara dissects the workings of the imperialist system with scientific clarity, unflinching truthfulness, and biting humor. Cuba has shown by its example, he says, that "a people can liberate themselves and keep themselves free." $15

MAURICE BISHOP SPEAKS

THE GRENADA REVOLUTION AND ITS OVERTHROW, 1979–83

The triumph of the 1979 revolution in the Caribbean island of Grenada had "importance for all struggles around the world," said Maurice Bishop, its central leader. Invaluable lessons from that workers and farmers government, overturned in a Stalinist-led coup in 1983, can be found in this collection of Bishop's speeches and interviews. $25

THOMAS SANKARA SPEAKS

THE BURKINA FASO REVOLUTION, 1983–87

Colonialism and imperialist domination have
left a legacy of hunger, illiteracy, and economic
backwardness in Africa. In 1983 the peasants and
workers of Burkina Faso established a popular
revolutionary government and began to combat the
causes of such devastation. Thomas Sankara, who
led that struggle, explains the example set for Africa
and the world. $24. Also in French.

ROSA LUXEMBURG SPEAKS

Edited by Mary-Alice Waters

From her political awakening as a high school
student in tsarist-occupied Poland until her
murder in 1919 during the German revolution,
Rosa Luxemburg acted and wrote as a proletarian
revolutionist. This collection of her writings
and speeches takes us inside the political battles
between revolution and class collaboration that still
shape the modern workers movement. $27

EUGENE V. DEBS SPEAKS

Speeches by the pioneer U.S. socialist agitator and
labor leader, jailed for opposing Washington's
imperialist aims in World War I. Debs speaks
out on capitalism and socialism, anti-immigrant
chauvinism, how anti-Black racism weakens the
labor movement, Rockefeller's massacre of striking
miners at Ludlow, Colorado, and more. $24

SOCIALISM ON TRIAL

James P. Cannon

The basic ideas of socialism, explained in testimony
during the 1941 trial of leaders of the Minneapolis
Teamsters union and the Socialist Workers Party
framed up and imprisoned under the notorious
Smith "Gag" Act during World War II. $16. Also in
Spanish.

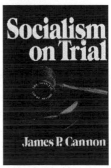

Capitalism's World Disorder
Working-Class Politics at the Millennium
JACK BARNES

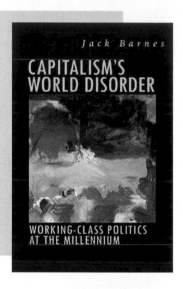

The social devastation and financial panic, the coarsening of politics, the cop brutality and acts of imperialist aggression accelerating around us—all are the product not of something gone wrong with capitalism but of its lawful workings. Yet the future can be changed by the united struggle and selfless action of workers and farmers conscious of their power to transform the world. $24. Also in Spanish and French.

The Changing Face of U.S. Politics
Working-Class Politics and the Trade Unions
JACK BARNES

Building the kind of party working people need to prepare for coming class battles through which they will organize and strengthen the unions, as they revolutionize themselves and all society. A handbook for those repelled by the class inequalities, racism, women's oppression, cop violence, and wars inherent in capitalism, for those who are seeking the road toward effective action to overturn that exploitative system and join in reconstructing the world on new, socialist foundations. $24. Also in Spanish, French, and Swedish.

The Communist Manifesto
KARL MARX AND FREDERICK ENGELS

Founding document of the modern working-class movement, published in 1848. Explains why communism is not a set of preconceived principles but the line of march of the working class toward power, "springing from an existing class struggle, a historical movement going on under our very eyes." $5. Also in Spanish.

Fighting Racism in World War II

C.L.R. JAMES, GEORGE BREITMAN,
EDGAR KEEMER, AND OTHERS

An account of struggles against lynch-mob terror and racist discrimination in U.S. war industries, the armed forces, and society as a whole from 1939 to 1945, taken from the pages of the socialist newsweekly, the *Militant*. These struggles helped lay the basis for the mass civil rights movement of the subsequent two decades. $22

Problems of Women's Liberation

EVELYN REED

Six articles explore the social and economic roots of women's oppression from prehistoric society to modern capitalism and point the road forward to emancipation. $15

Notebook of an Agitator

From the Wobblies to the Fight against the Korean War and McCarthyism

JAMES P. CANNON

Articles spanning four decades of working-class battles—defending IWW frame-up victims and Sacco and Vanzetti; 1934 Minneapolis Teamsters strikes; battles on the San Francisco waterfront; labor's fight against the McCarthyite witch-hunt; and much more. $26

Teamster Rebellion

FARRELL DOBBS

The 1934 strikes that built the industrial union movement in Minneapolis and helped pave the way for the CIO, recounted by a central leader of that battle. The first in a four-volume series on the class-struggle leadership of the strikes and organizing drives that transformed the Teamsters union in much of the Midwest into a fighting social movement and pointed the road toward independent labor political action. $19. Also in Spanish.

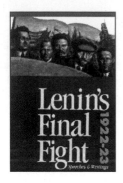

Lenin's Final Fight
Speeches and Writings, 1922–23
V.I. LENIN

In the early 1920s Lenin waged a political battle in the Communist Party leadership in the USSR to maintain the course that had enabled workers and peasants to overthrow the tsarist empire, carry out the first social-ist revolution, and begin building a world communist movement. The issues posed in this fight—from the leadership's class composition, to the worker-peasant alliance and battle against national oppression—remain central to world politics today. $21. Also in Spanish.

By Any Means Necessary
MALCOLM X

"Why should we do the dirtiest jobs for the lowest pay? I'm telling you we do it because we have a rotten system. It's a political and economic system of exploitation, of outright humiliation, degradation, discrimination."—Malcolm X, June 1964. $16

Cointelpro
The FBI's Secret War on Political Freedom
NELSON BLACKSTOCK

The decades-long covert spying and disruption program directed at socialists and activists in the Black and anti-Vietnam War movements. Includes FBI documents. $16

The Working Class and the Transformation of Learning
The Fraud of Education Reform under Capitalism
JACK BARNES

"Until society is reorganized so that education is a human activity from the time we are very young until the time we die, there will be no education worthy of working, creating humanity." $3. Also in Spanish, French, Swedish, and Icelandic.

Pathfinder Was Born with the October Revolution

MARY-ALICE WATERS

Pathfinder Press traces its continuity to those who launched the worldwide effort to defend and emulate the first socialist revolution—the October 1917 revolution in Russia. From the writings of Marx, Engels, Lenin, and Trotsky, to the words of Malcolm X, Fidel Castro, and Che Guevara, to those of James P. Cannon, Farrell Dobbs, and leaders of the communist movement in the U.S. today, Pathfinder books aim to "advance the understanding, confidence, and combativity of working people." $3. Also in Spanish and French.

Black Music, White Business

Illuminating the History and Political Economy of Jazz

FRANK KOFSKY

Probes the conflicts between the artistry of Black musicians and the control by largely white-owned businesses of jazz distribution—the recording companies, booking agencies, festivals, clubs, and magazines. $17

The Long View of History

GEORGE NOVACK

Why the struggle of working people for an end to oppression and exploitation is a realistic perspective built on sound scientific foundations, and why revolutionary change is fundamental to social and cultural progress. $7

The History of the Russian Revolution

LEON TROTSKY

A classic account of the social, economic, and political dynamics of the first socialist revolution as told by one of its central leaders. "The history of a revolution is for us first of all a history of the forcible entrance of the masses into the realm of rulership over their own destiny," Trotsky writes. Unabridged edition, 3 vols. in one. $36. Also in Russian.

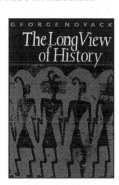

New International

A MAGAZINE OF MARXIST POLITICS AND THEORY

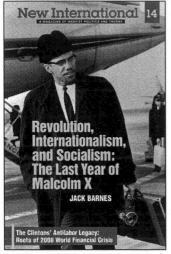

NEW INTERNATIONAL NO. 14

REVOLUTION, INTERNATIONALISM, AND SOCIALISM: THE LAST YEAR OF MALCOLM X

Jack Barnes

"To understand Malcolm's last year is to see how, in the imperialist epoch, revolutionary leadership of the highest political capacity, courage, and integrity converges with communism. That truth has even greater weight today as billions around the world, in city and countryside, from China to Brazil, are being hurled into the modern class struggle by the violent expansion of world capitalism."—Jack Barnes

Issue #14 also includes "The Clintons' Antilabor Legacy: Roots of the 2008 World Financial Crisis"; "The Stewardship of Nature Also Falls to the Working Class: In Defense of Land and Labor" and "Setting the Record Straight on Fascism and World War II." $14

NEW INTERNATIONAL NO. 12

CAPITALISM'S LONG HOT WINTER HAS BEGUN

Jack Barnes

and "Their Transformation and Ours,"
Resolution of the Socialist Workers Party

Today's sharpening interimperialist conflicts are fueled both by the opening stages of what will be decades of economic, financial, and social convulsions and class battles, and by the most far-reaching shift in Washington's military policy and organization since the U.S. buildup toward World War II. Class-struggle-minded working people must face this historic turning point for imperialism, and draw satisfaction from being "in their face" as we chart a revolutionary course to confront it. $16

ALL THESE ISSUES ARE ALSO AVAILABLE IN SPANISH AND MOST IN FRENCH AT
WWW.PATHFINDERPRESS.COM

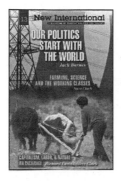

PATHFINDER AROUND THE WORLD

Visit our website for a complete list of titles and to place orders

www.pathfinderpress.com

PATHFINDER DISTRIBUTORS

UNITED STATES
(and Caribbean, Latin America, and East Asia)

Pathfinder Books, 306 W. 37th St., 10th Floor,
New York, NY 10018

CANADA

Pathfinder Books, 7105 St. Hubert, Suite 106F,
Montreal, QC H2S 2N1

UNITED KINGDOM
(and Europe, Africa, Middle East, and South Asia)

Pathfinder Books, First Floor, 120 Bethnal Green Road
(entrance in Brick Lane), London E2 6DG

SWEDEN

Pathfinder böcker, Bildhuggarvägen 17, S-121 44 Johanneshov

AUSTRALIA
(and Southeast Asia and the Pacific)

Pathfinder, Level 1, 3/281-287 Beamish St., Campsie, NSW 2194
Postal address: P.O. Box 164, Campsie, NSW 2194

NEW ZEALAND

Pathfinder, 7 Mason Ave. (upstairs), Otahuhu, Auckland
Postal address: P.O. Box 3025, Auckland 1140

PATHFINDER READERS CLUB • CLUB DE LECTORES

NAME
NOMBRE

EXPIRATION DATE • FECHA QUE VENCE:

Valid at Pathfinder book centers and online
Válida en centros de libros Pathfinder y en línea
www.pathfinderpress.com

Join the Pathfinder Readers Club

to get 15% discounts on all Pathfinder titles
and bigger discounts on special offers.
Sign up at www.pathfinderpress.com
or through the distributors above.